Science Projects, Grades

Table of Contents

Introduction 2
FOSS Correlation 3
Types of Projects 4
Science Fair Checklist 6
The Scientific Method 7
Your Science Fair Project 8
Science Fair Notebook 9
Presenting the Project 10

Unit 1: Earth Science

Sample Earth Science Project 11
How Hard Are Minerals? 12
Do the Continents Fit Together? 13
What Are Faults? 14
Does the Earth's Crust Move? 15
Can You Make a Mountain? 16
How Do Glaciers Change the Landscape? 17
Does the Earth's Crust Wear Away? 18
How Can Erosion Be Slowed? 19
What Happens at the Mid-Ocean Ridges? 20
How Can the Ocean Floor Be Measured? 21
How Can the Ocean Bottom Be Explored? 22
How Do Ocean Currents Behave? 23
How Does Salt Affect the Density of Water? 24
What Happens When Waves Meet? 25
Does Water Pressure Increase with Depth? 26
Lighter Than Water? 27
What Is the Greenhouse Effect? 28
Can the Sun's Energy Be Trapped? 29
Can Solar Energy Cook Food? 30
Can You Record Changes in Humidity? 32
Can You Make a Compass? 34
How Does the Moon Revolve Around the Earth? 35
How Do the Stars Look from Space? 36

Unit 2: Life Science

Sample Life Science Project 37
How Do You Know If a Food Contains Starch? 38
How Good Is Your Sense of Taste? 39
How Can You Change Your Pulse Rate? 40
What Is Your Lung Capacity? 41
Does Holding Your Breath Change the Amounts of
　　Oxygen and Carbon Dioxide You Exhale? 42
How Far Apart Are Nerve Cells? 43
How Does Skin Protect Against Infection? 44
How Good Is Your Short-Term Memory? 45
Can Inherited Traits Be Affected by the Environment? 46

Can You Select Traits to Pass On? 47
How Does a Caterpillar Metamorphose? 48
How Do Some Animals Insulate
Themselves from Heat? 49
Can You Make a Microscope? 50
Are You a Scientist? 51
What Can You Observe in Onion Skin Cells? 52
What Do Some Kinds of Protists Look Like? 53
Why Do Living Things Need Food? 54
How Are Fruit Seeds Alike and Different? 55
What Are Tropisms? 56
Do You Pollute? 58
What Are Decomposers? 60
Does Composting Really Work? 62

Unit 3: Physical Science

Sample Physical Science Project 63
How Can You Reduce Heat Loss? 64
How Do Crystals Form? 65
What Is the Boiling Point of a Liquid? 66
Does the Amount of Matter
　　Change After a Chemical Reaction? 67
How Can You Identify a Chemical Reaction? 68
What Is Combustion? 70
What Substance Is Needed for Burning? 71
How Can You Do Secret Writing? 72
What Are Acids and Bases? 73
What Is a Solution? 74
What Is Chromatography? 75
How Can the Rate at Which a
　　Substance Dissolves Be Changed? 76
What Is Distillation? 78
What Is Archimedes' Principle? 79
How Can You Compare the Inertia of Two Objects? . .80
What Are Balanced and Unbalanced Forces? 82
What Do Newton's Laws Have to Do with Seatbelt
　　Laws? 83
How Does Mass Affect Acceleration? 84
Can You Observe the Direction of Opposite Forces? . .86
Do Pulleys Make Work Easier? 87
How Can You Compare Forces? 88
Can You Make a Magnet? 90
How Do Nonmagnetic Materials Affect a Magnet? . . .91
Is It a Conductor or an Insulator? 92
What Is a Fuse? .94
What Is a Series Circuit? 95
What Is a Parallel Circuit? 96

Introduction

We arise in a new world every day. Our lives are caught in a whirlwind of change. New wonders are discovered on a daily basis. Technology is carrying us rapidly into the 21st century. How will our children keep pace with this constant change? We must provide them with the tools necessary to journey confidently into the future. Those tools can be found in a sound science education. One guidepost to a good foundation in science is the Full Option Science System™ (FOSS) Standards. This book adheres to these standards.

Young students are interested in almost everything around them—the Earth and sky, plants and animals, and the way things work. They should be encouraged to observe their world, the things in it, and their neighbors in the sky. They should take note of the properties of the Earth and its inhabitants and then try to develop their own explanation of why things are the way they are. A basic understanding of science boosts students' understanding of the world around them.

But knowledge without application would be wasted effort. Students should be encouraged to participate in their school science fair. To help facilitate this, *Science Projects* is packed with a variety of projects that students can do easily.

Organization

Science Projects is a handy companion to the regular science curriculum. It is divided into three units: Earth Science; Life Science; and Physical Science. Each unit contains a variety of science projects to spark the interest of science students and to reinforce students' knowledge and understanding of basic principles of science and the world around them.

The introductory section of the book contains several handy forms, charts, and schedules that will help a student to organize and conduct a project more efficiently. The introductory section also contains a correlation of the projects to the FOSS standards.

Developing a Project

An understanding of science is best promoted by hands-on experience. It is essential that students be given sufficient concrete examples of scientific concepts. Appropriate props can be bought or made from common everyday objects. Most of the projects can be completed with materials easily accessible to the students.

To help students develop a viable project, consider these guidelines:

1. Decide whether to do individual or group projects.
2. Help students choose a topic that interests them and that is manageable. Be sure a project is appropriate for a student's grade level and ability. Otherwise, that student might become frustrated. This does not mean that you should discourage a student's scientific curiosity. However, some projects are just not appropriate.
3. Encourage students to develop questions and to talk about their questions in class.
4. Help students to decide on one question or problem.
5. Help students to design a logical process for developing the project. Stress that the acquisition of materials is an important part of the project. Some projects also require strict schedules, so students must be willing and able to carry through with the process.
6. Remind students that the Scientific Method will help them to organize their thoughts and activities. Students should keep track of the resources used, whether they are people or print materials. Encourage students to use the Internet to do research on their project.
7. Be sure that you are familiar with the school's science-fair guidelines. Some schools, for example, do not allow glass or any electrical or flammable projects. An exhibit also is usually restricted to three or four feet of table space.

Judging

Inform students that a science project is usually judged using three criteria:

1. Exhibition Construction and Display: Creativity, neatness, organization, visual appeal, workmanship, and clarity
2. Exhibit Notebook: Thoroughness, scientific thought, investigative skills, organization and presentation of data, resources
3. Knowledge of Topic: Accuracy and completeness of information, clarity of data and results, understanding of topic, oral presentation

FOSS Correlation

Earth Science

Landforms Module

(Erosion; contour; landforms; elevation; topography)

11, 12, 13, 14, 15, 16, 17, 18, 19, 20, 21, 22, 23, 24, 25, 26, 27, 34

Solar Energy Module

(Solar energy; absorption; energy transfer; insulation)

28, 29, 30, 31, 32, 33, 64

Life Science

Environments Module

(Environment; organisms; preferred environment; adaptation; tolerance)

28, 37, 46, 47, 48, 49, 53, 55, 56, 57, 58, 59, 60, 61, 62

Food and Nutrition Module

(Acid; carbohydrate; nutrient; nutrition; metabolism; chemical reaction)

38, 39, 40, 42, 44, 54, 72

Physical Science

Mixtures and Solutions Module

(Crystals; dissolving; mixture; solution; evaporation; chemical reaction)

63, 65, 66, 67, 68, 69, 70, 71, 73, 74, 75, 76, 77, 78

Levers and Pulleys Module

(Fulcrum; lever; force; effort; pulleys; simple machine)

80, 81, 82, 83, 84, 85, 86, 87, 88, 89, 90, 91, 92, 93

Scientific Reasoning

Scientific Inquiry Module

(Variables; cause and effect; tolerance; graphing)

11, 13, 14, 15, 16, 17, 18, 21, 22, 23, 29, 32, 33, 37, 40, 41, 42, 43, 46, 50, 54, 56, 59, 60, 64, 66, 68, 69, 70, 71,

72, 73, 74, 75, 76, 77, 79, 83, 84, 85, 90, 95, 96

Types of Projects

A Collection Using Classifying

In a collection, you place items into groups according to their similar properties. The items should be science objects that you have collected. Your collection should not include stamps, coins or things that other people have collected. Decide carefully on the categories, or groups, in which you will place the items. Be sure to have several objects in each category. You should be able to explain how you grouped the objects when you present your project to the judges. For example, you might group rocks according to their color, their sparkle, or their source.

Each item on display should have a name or description. Your project should include the collection, a project notebook, and a posterboard display giving this information:

TITLE of the collection
INFORMATION about the collection
CLASSIFICATION SCHEME of the collected items

Examples of collections
feathers; eggshells; bird nests; seeds from grasses; pieces of bark; leaves; fossils; empty insect nests.

An Exhibit That Gives Information

An exhibit can be a model, a demonstration, or a display with a report. The report part of this project is an essay, with pictures, that gives information about your exhibit. Make the exhibit and write the report yourself. Use several sources for the information in your exhibit. Your report should be clear and factual. Be able to explain your exhibit to the judges.

Your project should include the exhibit, a project notebook, and a posterboard display giving this information:

TITLE of the exhibit
WRITTEN INFORMATION about the exhibit (may include diagrams)
EXPLANATION of what the exhibit shows
REFERENCES (books, articles, Internet sites, or resource people used)

Examples of exhibits
Demonstration: You could demonstrate how light reflects off different things. You might set up mirrors and show how a beam of light from a flashlight bounces from one mirror to the next. Your report should explain that light travels in straight lines.

Model: You could make a cutaway model of the Earth out of clay. Labels could show the layers of the Earth, and your report could give information about each level.

Display: You could make a display about birds, showing pictures of different kinds of birds. Your report could tell where the birds live, what they eat, and some interesting habits of the birds.

Types of Projects, page 2

An Experiment That Answers a Question

An experiment tries to answer a question. Good experiment questions are about things you think might be true. What you think is true is called your "hypothesis." Then, design an experiment or test that will show if your hypothesis is correct. Your experiment procedure should use the Scientific Method. Show samples, photos, or other proof that you really did the experiment. Show your "Conclusion" in charts or graphs. Read books to get more information about your topic. Use your own ideas and your own words. Be able to explain your experiment to the judges.

Your project should include the experiment equipment and proof, a project notebook, and a posterboard display giving this information:

TITLE of the experiment
PROBLEM: What question are you trying to answer?
HYPOTHESIS: What do you think the answer to your question is?

EXPERIMENTATION: What materials did you use to carry out the experiment? What did you do in your investigation?
OBSERVATION: What did you observe during the experiment? Include your notes.
CONCLUSION: What happened in the experiment? What is the answer to the question in your "Problem"? How do you explain your results? (Use tables of data or graphs.)
COMPARISON: Does your conclusion agree with your hypothesis? If so, you have shown that your hypothesis was correct.
PRESENTATION: Prepare a presentation or report to share your findings.
RESOURCES: Include a list of resources used. Give credit to books or people that helped you with your work.

Examples of subjects for experiments

Do ants like diet soda? Does sound travel at the same speed through all objects? Does warm water freeze faster than cold water?

Name _____   Date _____

Science Fair Checklist

The science fair at your school is a good place to show your science skills and knowledge. You need to think about your project carefully so that it will show your best work. Use the Scientific Method to help you to organize your project. Here are some other things to consider:

PROJECT TITLE _____

Working Plan	Date Due	Date Completed	Teacher Initials
1. Select topic			
2. Explore resources			
3. Start notebook			
4. Form hypothesis			
5. Find materials			
6. Investigate			
7. Prepare results			
8. Prepare summary			
9. Plan your display			
10. Construct your display			
11. Complete notebook			
12. Prepare for judging			

Write a brief paragraph describing the hypothesis, materials, and procedures you will include in your exhibit. Be sure to plan your project carefully. Get all the materials and resources you need beforehand. A good presentation should have plenty of visual aids, so use pictures, charts, and other things to make your project easier to understand.

Be sure to follow all the rules for your school science fair. Also, be prepared for the judging part. The judges will want to see a clear and thorough presentation of your data and resources. They will also want to see that you understand your project and can tell them about it clearly and thoroughly. Good luck!

Name _____   Date _____

The Scientific Method

Did you know you think and act like a scientist? You can prove it by following these steps when you have a problem. The steps are called the Scientific Method.

1. PROBLEM: Identify a problem or question to investigate.

_____

_____

2. HYPOTHESIS: Tell what you think will be the result of your investigation or activity.

_____

_____

3. EXPERIMENTATION: Perform the investigation or activity.

_____

4. OBSERVATION: Make observations, and take notes about what you observe.

_____

_____

_____

5. CONCLUSION: Draw conclusions from what you have observed.

_____

_____

_____

6. COMPARISON: Does your conclusion agree with your hypothesis? If so, you have shown that your hypothesis was correct. If not, you need to decide why your hypothesis was incorrect and then revise it.

_____

7. PRESENTATION: Prepare a presentation or report to share your findings.

8. RESOURCES: Include a list of resources used. You need to give credit to people or books you used to help you with your work.

_____

_____

Name _____   Date _____

Your Science Fair Project

You have just picked a topic that you want to know more about. Use this sheet to record information about your project.

Project topic _____

Questions I have about my topic _____

_____

_____

Materials I will need for my project _____

_____

How I will set up my project _____

_____

_____

Draw a sketch to show how your finished project will look.

Observations I made during my project _____

_____

_____

What I discovered about my topic _____

_____

Science Fair Notebook

The science fair notebook helps you to organize all your information about your project. Work hard to prepare a neat, carefully arranged notebook.

In your notebook, include as many of these parts as possible:

Title Page
This should include the title of the project, the type of project, the student's name, the teacher's name, and the date of the science fair.

Table of Contents
This is a listing of the parts inside the notebook and their page numbers.

Hypothesis
If you are doing an experiment, state the hypothesis and include an explanation of why you chose to test this hypothesis.

Materials
This page contains a detailed listing of all materials used in the project. Be as specific as possible.

Research
This section should include all the information you collected to prepare the project. Include a summary for each source listed in the Resources Used section.

Experimentation
If you are doing an experiment, include all the steps taken in testing your hypothesis. The information should be clear and thorough. Each step should include all observations, notes, and supporting graphs, charts, drawings, or photos.

Conclusion
In this section, you should analyze the notes collected during the experiment. Then, you should state whether the results support the hypothesis.

Resources Used
List all the books, magazines, newspapers, or interviews that you summarized in the Research section.

Neatly arrange all your information in a binder or folder. You might also include the title of your project on the cover.

Presenting the Project

An important part of the science project is the presentation. You must display your project so others can understand your work. Your display should be neatly done and sturdy enough to last through the science fair. Your display should be designed so the materials and equipment are not dangerous.

Be sure that you know the rules of your school science fair. You will be assigned an amount of space for your project, often 2 to 4 feet of table space. Check to see if your project can use electricity or glass containers.

Your display can be made of 2 to 4 panels of a sturdy material such as cardboard, pegboard, or wood. The panels should be able to stand and support themselves after being fastened together with tape or hinges.

All titles should be done neatly and be self-explanatory. The title of the project should be placed across the top of the middle panel. Subtitles should follow the Scientific Method, and should include such headings as problem, hypothesis, experiment, methods, results, and conclusion.

Be sure your charts and graphs are neatly done. Color graphs are recommended. Photographs, computer graphics, and drawings should be neatly arranged. Label all the materials on display.

Study the display below for ideas.

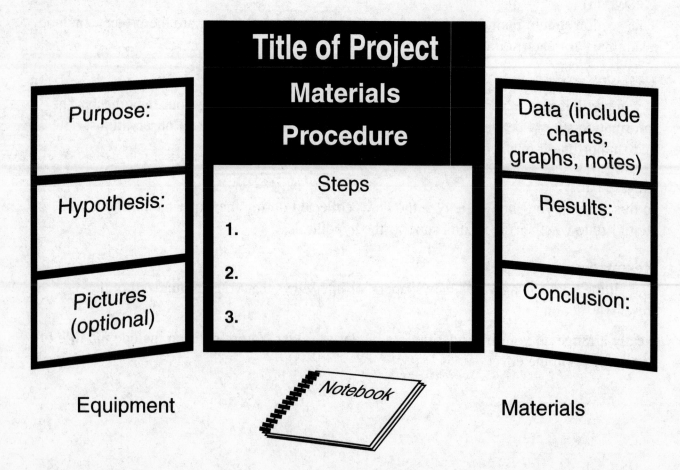

Name _____   Date _____

Earth Science Project

A science fair project can help you to understand the world around you better. Choose a topic that interests you. Then, use the Scientific Method to develop your project. Here's an example:

1. **PROBLEM:** How does cold water affect water under the surface of the ocean?

2. **HYPOTHESIS:** Cold water causes currents.

3. **EXPERIMENTATION:** Materials: baking dish; 2 glasses; tap water; warm water; ice water; red and blue food coloring; spoon

   Fill the dish with tap water. Fill one glass with very warm water and the other with ice water. Put red food coloring in the warm water and blue food coloring in the ice water. Mix each with a spoon. Pour the warm water slowly into one end of the dish. Pour the cold water slowly into the other end. Observe the movement.

4. **OBSERVATION:** The red and blue colored waters mix with the water in the dish. The cold, blue water moves underneath the warm, red water.

5. **CONCLUSION:** When cold water mixes with warmer water, a current is formed.

6. **COMPARISON:** The conclusion and the hypothesis agree.

7. **PRESENTATION:** Demonstrate the experiment for the judges, and explain what caused the water movement.

8. **RESOURCES:** Name the books you used to learn about ocean currents. Tell who helped you get materials and set up the experiment.

MORE IDEAS

1. What causes a flood?
2. What is wind chill?
3. What would happen if the Earth lost its gravitational pull on the Moon?
4. What causes icebergs?
5. What is nuclear fusion?

Name _____   Date _____

How Hard Are Minerals?

Rocks are made up of minerals. Minerals are identified by the properties they possess. These properties include how minerals split, their hardness, their specific gravity, and the streak they leave when rubbed against a hard white surface. Sometimes color is also used to identify minerals.

Look at the table. It rates ten kinds of minerals by hardness. It is known as Mohs' Hardness Scale. How hard is a mineral? You can check.

MOHS' HARDNESS SCALE

MATERIALS

6 different minerals
a piece of tile

Mineral	Hardness Rating
talc	1
gypsum	2
calcite	3
fluorite	4
apatite	5
orthoclase	6
quartz	7
topaz	8
corundum	9
diamond	10

Procedure

1. Label the minerals **A** through **F**. With mineral A, scratch the surface of mineral B. With B, scratch the surface of A. If A scratched B, then A is harder than B. If B scratched A, then B is harder than A. Record your results.

2. Repeat the scratch test with all the minerals. The softest mineral can be scratched by all the others. Record your results.

3. With mineral A, draw a line on the unglazed side of the tile. Compare the color of the streak with the color of the mineral.

4. Repeat the streak test with the other five minerals. Compare the colors of the minerals and their streaks. Record your results.

Drawing Conclusions

1. Which mineral was the hardest? Which was the softest? How do you know?
2. What is the color of each mineral? What is the color of its streak?

Do the Continents Fit Together?

Were all the world's land masses once joined together? Alfred Wegener believed that all the continents fit together long ago, about 225 million years. He thought there was only one great land mass, called Pangea. Then, the continents drifted apart. Could his theory be correct? If it is, the edges of the continents should match up like the pieces of a worn jigsaw puzzle. Here's an activity to see if Wegener might have been right.

MATERIALS

world map
scissors
construction paper
glue

Procedure

1. Cut out all the continents on the world map below. Be careful using the scissors.
2. Fit all the continents together like the pieces of a puzzle. Do they fit together?
3. Glue the pieces onto the sheet of construction paper. Be sure you glue them so they fit together as well as possible.
4. In your report, write a paragraph describing what you think Pangea was like. Then, include your supercontinent and report in your display.
5. You may want to do more research on the theory of continental drift.

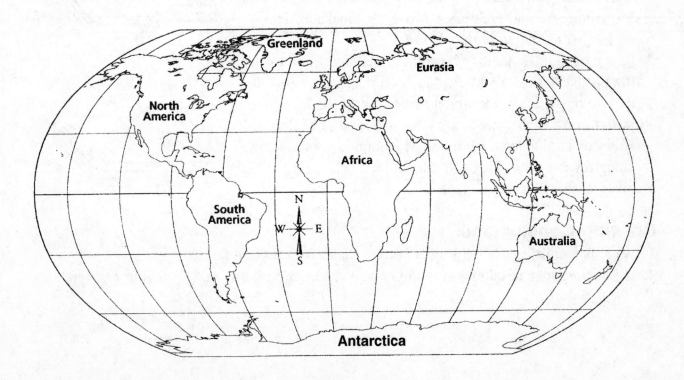

What Are Faults?

Faults are breaks in the Earth's crust. The rock walls on either side of a fault can slip past each other when forces in the Earth move them. This movement is a major cause of earthquakes. The three major kinds of faults are lateral faults, normal faults, and reverse faults. The difference between these faults is the way in which the rock walls move past each other. You can demonstrate each kind of fault.

MATERIALS

2 blocks of clay

Procedure

1. Lateral Fault: Pressures under the Earth's surface sometimes push pieces of the crust that are next to each other in opposite directions. The rock walls slip sideways past each other, forming a lateral fault. Move the clay blocks alongside each other as shown in the picture.

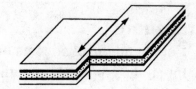

2. Normal Fault: Forces within the Earth sometimes push one rock wall up while pulling the wall next to it down. When the rock walls pull away from each other, the rock eventually breaks, forming a normal fault line. One of the walls slides downward past the other. Mountain ranges can form along normal fault lines. Move the blocks against each other as shown in the picture.

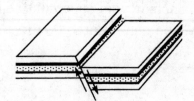

3. Reverse Fault: In addition to pulling rock apart, forces in the Earth can push rock together. This pressure causes the rock to break apart, forming a reverse fault. Rock walls push toward each other along a reverse fault line. One wall slides upward against the other. Mountain ranges can form along reverse fault lines, too. Move the blocks against each other as shown in the picture.

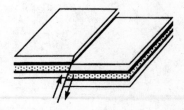

Drawing Conclusions

1. What is the difference between a normal fault and a reverse fault?
2. Is it a good idea to build a building or a road near a fault line? Explain your answer.

Name _____   Date _____

Does the Earth's Crust Move?

Scientists believe that Earth's crust is broken into 10 or 12 pieces, called plates. When the plates move, the continents move, too. Scientists think that the plates can move in three ways. They can collide, spread, or slip. These movements occur at the boundary lines between the plates. These boundary lines are called faults.

When two plates push against each other, they collide. The thin part of one plate slowly pushes its way under the thick part of another plate. The upper plate then rises. This is how some mountains are formed. Earthquakes are also common where plates collide.

Two plates can move apart, or spread. This spreading causes magma (molten rock) to squeeze up between the plates. The magma then cools and hardens into new crust. Volcanoes and earthquakes are very common where plates move apart.

Two plates can also slide past each other, or slip, causing a great grinding. The San Andreas Fault in California divides two plates. One is called the North American Plate, and the other is the Pacific Plate. These two plates slide against each other often, so that earthquakes are common in California.

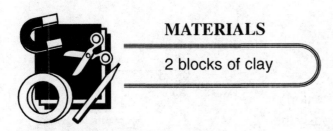

MATERIALS

2 blocks of clay

1. Draw arrows on the diagrams below to show the three ways that plates can move. Include the pictures with your display. Under each picture, write an example of what might happen when the plates move.
2. Use the blocks of clay to demonstrate the three ways that plates can move.
3. Do research on famous earthquakes. Include details in your report.

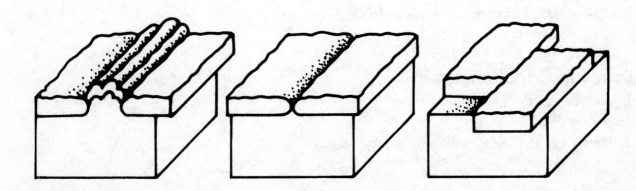

Can You Make a Mountain?

The movement of the crust plates can cause mountains to form in three ways. When two plates collide, the crust is bent and squeezed. Squeezing causes the layers of rock to fold, forming folded mountains.

When rocks are squeezed, they do not always bend. Sometimes they crack and tilt, forming fault-block mountains. These mountains have large blocks of rock divided by faults.

When the plates spread, magma may force its way under layers of rock. It pushes in between the layers, bending the layers above. This crust action causes dome-shaped mountains. This activity will show you how each type is formed.

MATERIALS

3 colors of clay
2 wood blocks
plastic knife
golf ball

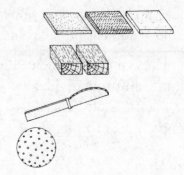

Procedure

1. Make 3 rectangular stacks of clay, each having 3 different colored layers. The layers are like layers of rock.
2. Place one stack of clay flat on a table. Put a wood block at each end of the clay stack. Slowly push the wood blocks together. Watch what happens. What kind of mountain is formed?
3. Cut the second stack of clay in half. Hold one half steady as you slide the other half along the cut edge. Look at the layers of clay. What kind of mountain is formed this way?
4. Mold the third stack of clay over the golf ball. Gently remove the golf ball. Then cut the stack of clay in half. Notice what happens to the layers of clay. What kind of mountain is formed this way?

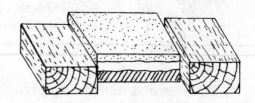

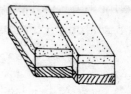

Drawing Conclusions

1. Are mountains formed quickly or over a long period of time?
2. How were the landforms in your area formed?

How Do Glaciers Change the Landscape?

A glacier is a large body of moving ice and snow. Over time, snow is packed layer upon layer. The lower layers turn to ice. More and more layers form on the glacier. Finally, the glacier is so heavy that it begins to move. It flows downhill from mountains to lower ground. Glaciers erode the land by breaking rocks and carrying them away. This activity shows how a glacier can change the landscape.

MATERIALS

gravel   pan   sand   pebbles   water
small plastic container with tight lid

Procedure

1. Put a handful of gravel in the small plastic container. Add water almost to the top of the container. Close the lid tightly, and put the container in the freezer overnight.
2. When the water is frozen solid, remove the ice from the container. In what ways is the ice like a glacier?
3. Place the ice in the pan $\frac{1}{3}$ filled with sand and pebbles. Press firmly on the ice as you push it through the sand and pebbles.

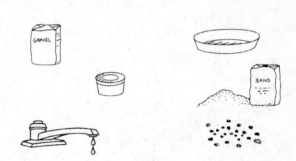

Drawing Conclusions

1. How does pressing down on the ice make it act like a glacier?
2. How does the ice and gravel mixture change the sand and pebbles?
3. Do you think the same changes would happen without the gravel in the ice?

MORE IDEAS

1. Include your setup with your display.
2. Do research on areas of North America where the landscape was carved by glaciers.

Name _____   Date _____

Does the Earth's Crust Wear Away?

Water weathers rocks physically. In this activity, you will observe what happens to water when it freezes and learn why it can break rocks apart.

MATERIALS

water
masking tape
2 plastic margarine containers with lids

Procedure

1. Fill one plastic container to the top with water. Cover this container with its lid. Place masking tape across the lid to hold it down tightly.
2. Cover the other empty container. Place the masking tape across its lid.
3. Place each container in the freezer for several hours.
4. Remove the plastic containers from the freezer.

Drawing Conclusions

1. What happened to the containers?
2. What do you think would happen if water seeped into a rock and froze?

MORE IDEAS

1. Include your setup with your display.
2. Do research to learn more about different kinds of physical and chemical weathering. Include your findings in your report.

How Can Erosion Be Slowed?

Erosion is the breaking down and carrying away of soil and rocks. Valuable nutrients can be lost when farmland erodes. People can slow down erosion. Try this experiment to see one way.

MATERIALS

2 large, rectangular cake pans
sandy soil, 4 liters
2 books
sprinkling can
water

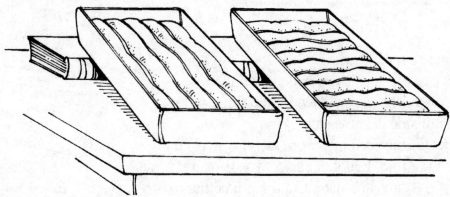

Procedure

1. Pour some soil into each cake pan, and spread it evenly. Each pan represents a farmer's field.
2. Make furrows, or grooves, across the length of one pan.
3. Make furrows across the width of the other pan.
4. Raise one end of each pan by leaning it against a book. Predict which field will erode faster.
5. Then, use a sprinkling can to pour water over the raised end of each field.

Drawing Conclusions

1. What do you see happening?
2. What is causing the soil to erode?
3. Draw a circle around the field that eroded faster. Was your prediction correct?

MORE IDEAS

1. Include your setup with your display.
2. Tell the judges your prediction. Then, do the experiment for the judges.
3. Do research to learn how farmers slow down erosion in their fields.

Name _____   Date _____

What Happens at the Mid-Ocean Ridges?

The Earth's crust is spreading apart about 2 cm a year at the mid-ocean ridges. You can make a model to show that rocks farther away from a ridge are older than those closer to the ridge.

MATERIALS

sheet of white paper
stacks of books
pen or pencil
ruler

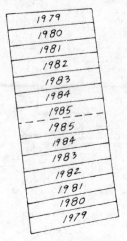

Procedure

1. Fold the paper in half. Starting at the fold, use your ruler to measure off lines 2 cm wide down the right-hand side of the paper. Then do the same thing to the left-hand side of the paper.

2. Write the date of the current year in the two strips on either side of the fold. Label the next two strips on either side with last year's date. Continue labeling each pair of strips with the previous year's date.

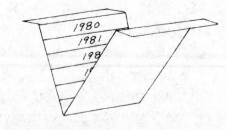

3. Push two equal stacks of books together. Following the same fold line, refold the paper so the writing is folded inside. The strips with the same dates will touch each other. Put the paper between the books. The paper represents the hot magma that rises up at the mid-ocean ridge and forms new rock. The numbers represent the years in which the rocks formed.

4. Slowly pull the edges of the paper away from the center. Note the dates on the strips when they appear between the "ridge." Where are the oldest dates? Where are the more recent dates? What force moves the older rock to its new position?

5. Pull the paper the rest of the way out. Did strips with matching dates move at the same rate?

This model shows how hot magma moves up out of the crust. As it cools, it is pushed away from the crack by new magma rising up. The rocks are pushed in both directions at the same rate.

How Can the Ocean Floor Be Measured?

How deep is the ocean? The ocean floor has valleys and mountains, slopes and plains, just like the continents. This activity will give you one way of measuring the ocean bottom.

MATERIALS

gravel   graph paper
water   aquarium
ruler

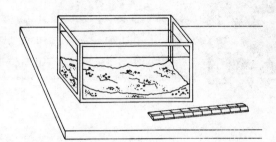

Procedure

1. Put the gravel in the bottom of the aquarium. Shape it to make a model of the four parts of the ocean bottom. Carefully fill the aquarium with water.

2. Hold the ruler straight up in the water at one end of your model. Measure how deep your "ocean" is.

3. On the graph, mark an X above "trial 1" opposite the number that shows the distance in centimeters between the ocean bottom and the water's surface.

4. Repeat Steps 2 and 3 for nine more trials, taking measurements from one end of the aquarium to the other.

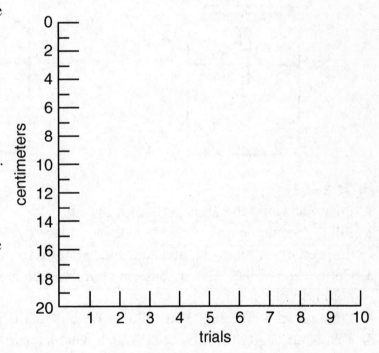

5. Draw a line that connects all the X marks on your graph. Label each part of the ocean bottom on your graph, too.

Drawing Conclusions

1. According to your graph, how deep is the ocean floor?
2. Are there any mountains? How tall are they?
3. In what ways is your model not like the ocean bottom? How could your model be improved?

MORE IDEAS

1. Include your setup with your display.
2. Do research on sonar and other methods of measuring the ocean bottom.

How Can the Ocean Bottom Be Explored?

A bathyscaphe is a device used to explore the ocean bottom. By building a Cartesian diver, you will observe how some bathyscaphes work.

MATERIALS

balloon	medicine dropper	scissors
glass jar	rubber band	water

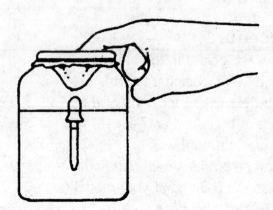

Procedure

1. Pour water into the glass jar until it is $\frac{3}{4}$ full.
2. Fill the medicine dropper with water and place it, tube end down, into the water. If the dropper sinks, remove it and adjust the water level in it until it floats.
3. Cut a piece of the balloon, and stretch it over the mouth of the jar. Use a rubber band to hold it in place.
4. Press down on the stretched balloon. Watch what happens to the medicine dropper.
5. Take your hand off the balloon. Watch what happens to the dropper.

Drawing Conclusions

1. What happened to the dropper when you pressed down on the balloon?
2. Why did the dropper sink?
3. How do you think this is similar to what a bathyscaphe does to sink into the ocean?

MORE IDEAS

1. Include your setup with your display.
2. Do research on other kinds of deep-sea diving vessels.

Name _____ Date _____

How Do Ocean Currents Behave?

Ocean currents can be caused by differences in ocean temperatures. In this activity, you will find out why.

MATERIALS

aquarium
2 thermometers
tape
water
watch
ice cube tinted with food coloring

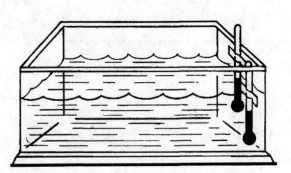

Temperature	Top	Bottom
At start		
1 minute		
2 minutes		
3 minutes		
4 minutes		

Procedure

1. Set up the aquarium and thermometers as shown in the drawing. Tape one thermometer to the inside of the aquarium so that it will measure the water temperature at the top of the aquarium. Tape the other thermometer so that it measures the water temperature at the bottom of the aquarium.
2. Fill the aquarium and read the temperature of the water near each thermometer. Record the temperatures on the chart.
3. Place the ice cube near the thermometer that measures the water temperature at the top of the aquarium.
4. Read the temperature of the water near each thermometer every minute for four minutes. Record the temperatures in the chart. Observe how the cold, colored water moves as the ice cube melts.

Drawing Conclusions

1. Which thermometer showed the greatest temperature change?
2. Why did the temperature decrease at the bottom of the aquarium when the ice cube was placed at the top?
3. How does this experiment relate to ocean currents?

How Does Salt Affect the Density of Water?

Density is the amount of mass in a certain volume. Suppose that two materials take up the same amount of space but have different masses. Then, these two materials would have different densities. The material with the greater mass has the greater density.

You can find out how salt affects the density of water. You can also see the effect of density on currents.

MATERIALS

2 identical measuring spoons
2 identical clear cups
blue food coloring
red food coloring

balance scale
eyedropper
wax pencil
measuring cup

salt
pencil
water

Procedure

1. Use the wax pencil to label the cups **Cup 1** and **Cup 2**. Label the spoons **S1** and **S2**. Always use S1 with Cup 1 and S2 with Cup 2. This will prevent accidentally adding extra salt to either cup.

2. Add 125 mL of water to each cup. Put one cup on each side of the balance scale. Do they have the same mass? (If the cups do not balance, adjust the volume of water until they do.) Remove the cups from the scale.

3. With S1, add 1 teaspoon of salt to Cup 1. Stir. With S2, add 4 teaspoons of salt to Cup 2. Stir.

4. Place the cups on the balance. Which cup has the greater mass? Why? Which cup has the greater density? Remove the cups from the scale.

5. Add 3 drops of red food coloring to Cup 1. Stir with S1. Add 3 drops of blue coloring to Cup 2. Stir with S2.

6. Add a dropperful of blue water from Cup 2 to one edge of the water in Cup 1. What happens? Why?

Drawing Conclusions

1. Which part of the oceans do you think are the saltier, the top or the bottom?

2. What effect does a difference in density have on ocean waters?

Name _____ Date _____

What Happens When Waves Meet?

What happens when two sets of waves meet each other? Do they transfer energy and scatter? Do they pass through each other? Do they join and make one big wave? To find out, try this activity.

MATERIALS

large, flat pan
water

Procedure

1. Fill the pan almost full of water.
2. Wait for the water to become still. Near one end of the pan, put your finger gently in the water. Take it out. How does the water move?
3. Wait for the water to become still again. Then, gently place a finger from one hand into one end of the pan. At the same time, place a finger from the other hand into the other end of the pan. Take your fingers out. What happens to the waves?

Drawing Conclusions

1. Is there a transfer of energy from one wave to another?
2. Do the waves join to become one wave?
3. What happens when the waves meet?

Light waves are like water waves. They do not crash when they come in contact. They pass through each other. They keep on going, without transferring energy.

MORE IDEAS

1. Include your setup with your display.
2. Do research on wave motion. Include your findings in your report.
3. Do research on large waves, such as tidal waves or tsunamis. Include the details in your report.

Name _____ Date _____

Does Water Pressure Increase with Depth?

How do we know that the deeper we go in water, the greater the pressure becomes? Here is a simple exercise you can do to answer that question.

MATERIALS

coffee can with three equal-sized holes (one hole at the bottom of the can, each of the other two holes 4 cm directly above the other)
large metal pan or flat plastic container
meter stick   tripod   water

Procedure

1. Place the tripod on a table, and place the coffee can on the tripod.
2. Place the pan against the tripod so that it can catch the water spurting from the holes in the can.
3. Place the meter stick inside the pan. The **0** end of the meter stick should be directly under the holes in the can.
4. Fill the can with water, and observe the stream of water spurting from each hole in the can.
5. Measure the distance each stream spurts from the can. Record your results in the chart.

Placement of hole	Distance water traveled
Top	
Middle	
Bottom	

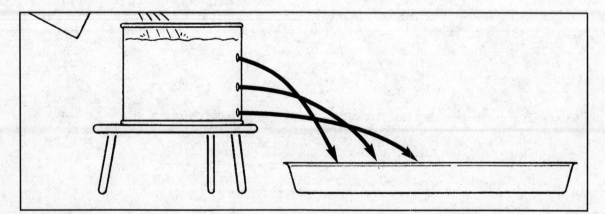

Drawing Conclusions

1. From what you have observed, at what level of the can do you think the pressure is greatest? Is it at the level of the top hole, the middle hole, or the bottom hole? Explain.
2. How does your data demonstrate that water pressure increases with depth?

Name _____   Date _____

Lighter Than Water?

You know that oil is lighter than water. You also know that warm air is lighter than cold air. Can one kind of water be lighter than another? Try this experiment to find out.

MATERIALS

3 colors of food coloring	salt	masking tape
3 drinking straws	tap water	measuring spoons
clear plastic glass	3 cups	marking pen

Procedure

1. Fill each cup half full of water. In one cup, add 2 teaspoons of salt to the water. Make a masking-tape label that tells how much salt you added, and attach it to the cup. Stir until the salt is dissolved.

2. Add 4 teaspoons of salt to another cup of water. Make a masking-tape label that records how much salt you added, and attach it to the cup. Stir until the salt is dissolved. Leave one cup with no salt.

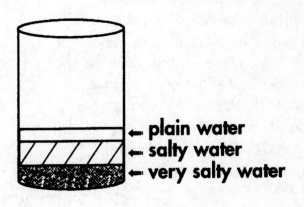

← plain water
← salty water
← very salty water

3. Add a few drops of a different food coloring to each cup. Stir the water in the cups.

4. Put a straw into the water containing 4 teaspoons of salt. Put your finger over the opening, and move the straw over the clear plastic glass. Let the water run into the clear glass. Using another straw, repeat the process for the water containing 2 teaspoons of salt. Carefully let the water run into the clear glass on top of the very salty water. Repeat the process with the plain water.

Drawing Conclusions

1. What can you tell about salty water from the diagram?
2. In an estuary, salt water from the ocean meets fresh water from a river. Where do you think the ocean water would be in an estuary, on the top or on the bottom?

Name _____ Date _____

What Is the Greenhouse Effect?

Have you ever noticed how hot the inside of a car gets in the sunlight? This is due to the greenhouse effect. Greenhouses are also heated by the Sun. Glass lets the Sun's rays through. Objects inside the greenhouse are heated by the Sun's rays. Then, the objects begin to radiate heat. This heat is trapped inside since it cannot easily pass through the glass.

Carbon dioxide in the air can act like the glass on a greenhouse to trap heat. Carbon dioxide in the air lets the rays of the Sun through. The Sun's rays heat the Earth. Some of this heat is

radiated into the air. Carbon dioxide then traps some of this radiated heat. Burning fossil fuels, such as oil, coal, and natural gas, increases the amount of carbon dioxide in the air. Scientists are worried that an increase in carbon dioxide in the air will increase the temperature of the air all over the world. Just a rise of a few degrees could cause the polar ice caps to melt. This would raise the sea level by as much as 120 m (400 ft). Coastal states would be flooded as a result.

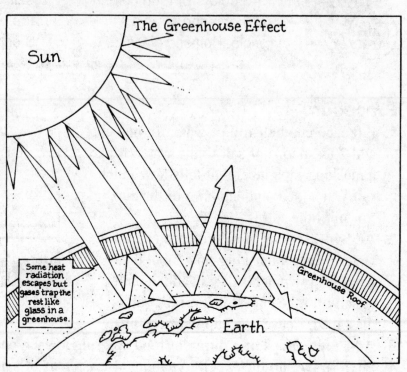

This activity will show you how the greenhouse effect works.

MATERIALS

a glass jar with a top
a thermometer
scissors
black paper

Procedure

1. Cut a disc out of the black paper to fit in the bottom of the jar.
2. Put the thermometer in the jar. Cover the jar, and put it in the sunlight.
3. Record the temperature after one hour.
4. Measure the air temperature in the place where the jar was.

Drawing Conclusions

1. Which temperature was higher? Explain.
2. What can be done to reduce the greenhouse effect?

Can the Sun's Energy Be Trapped?

People design and build strong houses for shelter. In cold climates, people need to heat their homes, too. Some people use the Sun's energy to warm their houses. To find out how the Sun's energy can be trapped, you can make a model of a solar collector.

MATERIALS

thermometer	water
black paint	large jar
2 empty tin cans (same size)	paint brush

Procedure

1. Paint the outside of one can with black paint. Let it dry.
2. Fill the large jar with cold water. Pour equal amounts of this water into both cans.
3. Place the cans side by side in a sunny spot. Be sure they are not near a radiator. Measure the temperature of water in both cans. Record your findings in the chart.
4. Measure the temperature of the air next to the cans. Record it in the chart.
5. Be sure that both cans are in the sunlight all day. Move them if necessary. After four hours, measure the temperatures again. Record your findings in the chart.

Water temperature	Unpainted can	Painted can	Air
at start of experiment			
temperature after 4 hours			

Drawing Conclusions

1. Which was warmer at the start, the temperature of the air or the temperature of the water?
2. What happened to the water temperature in the unpainted can?
3. What happened to the water temperature in the painted can?
4. In which can did the water temperature change more?
5. Where did the heat come from that heated the water?

Can Solar Energy Cook Food?

The amount of solar energy reaching the Earth is huge, but it is difficult to collect. Not only is much of it absorbed or reflected by the atmosphere, but also the heat and light that do reach the Earth are not concentrated. In this project, you will construct a device that collects and concentrates solar energy to use for cooking.

MATERIALS

1 shoebox	masking tape
aluminum foil	1 wire coat hanger
poster board or	1 hot dog
oatmeal container	scissors

Procedure

1. Make a trough to hold the hot dog while it cooks, either by cutting the oatmeal container in half lengthwise or by using the poster board. If you use the poster board, cut a rectangular piece of board 0.5 in. (12 mm) shorter than the length of the box and 3 in. (75 mm) wider than the box's width. Measure the box opening, then subtract 0.5 in. (12 mm) from its length and add 3 in. (75 mm) to its width.
CAUTION: Be careful when handling the scissors.

2. Hold the rectangle on end, and curve it to form the letter C. Trace the bottom edge of the curved poster board onto another piece (see the diagram).

3. Draw a line from one side to the other of the traced curve, then cut it out.

4. Use this as a pattern to trace and cut another. Each of these pieces should resemble a half-circle.

5. Again, hold the rectangle up to form a curve, and tape one of the half-circles to each end (see the diagram). This will form a kind of trough.

6. Cover the trough (made of either the oatmeal container or poster board) completely with aluminum foil, shiny side out. Try not to wrinkle the foil. Secure it in back of the trough with tape.

7. Carefully use a scissor point to make a small hole in the center of each end of the shoebox.

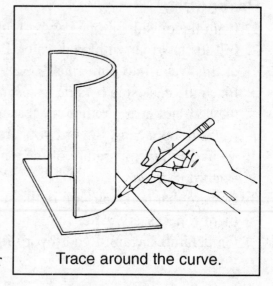

Trace around the curve.

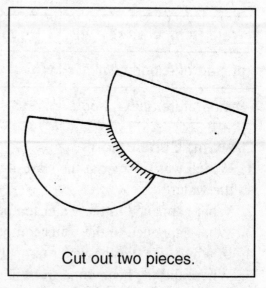

Cut out two pieces.

Can Solar Energy Cook Food?, page 2

8. Make holes in the center of each end of the aluminum-covered trough.

9. Have an adult straighten out the wire of the coat hanger, leaving the hook at one end.

10. Thread the straight end of the wire through the hole in one end of the shoebox from the outside in. Push it through only a short distance.

11. Set the trough into the box with its opening facing out.

12. Thread the hanger through the hole in this piece.

13. Push a hot dog up the length of the hanger. Keep pushing the hanger until it goes in the holes you placed on the other side of your cooker.

14. Take your cooker outside, and set it in a sunny spot. Turn the curved piece up and down until the Sun appears to be focused in the center. Put clear plastic wrap over the cooker to keep out dust and bugs.

15. Check your cooker several times over the next hour to see if your hot dog has cooked. Use the hook on the wire to turn it. CAUTION: Use an oven mitt to avoid burning your hand on the hot wire.

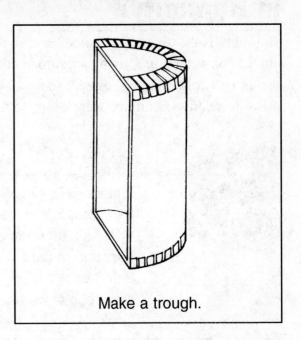

Make a trough.

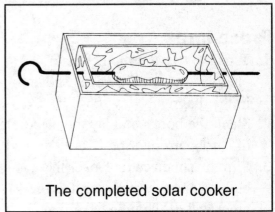

The completed solar cooker

Drawing Conclusions

1. What caused the hot dog to cook?
2. How could you increase the efficiency of your cooker?

MORE IDEAS

1. Try spray-painting the foil black or white. Investigate how this affects cooking times.

2. Test how the angle to the Sun affects the cooker. (Use a cooking thermometer to measure the temperature inside the cooker.)

3. Try making several cookers to see which shape works best (square, curved, or dish shaped).

Can You Record Changes in Humidity?

Humidity is the amount of water vapor in the air. Relative humidity is the amount of water vapor in the air compared to the amount of water vapor the air can hold. Meteorologists use a tool called a psychrometer to measure relative humidity. Here's how to make a simple psychrometer.

MATERIALS

2 pieces of stiff cardboard (23 x 30 cm)
8-cm piece of woven shoelace (forms a tube)
2 Celsius thermometers
transparent tape
2 or 3 books
small cup of water
clock

Procedure

1. Tape the two thermometers to one piece of cardboard, as shown in the diagram.

2. Stack the books and lay the piece of cardboard on top.

3. Slip the shoelace tube over the bulb of one thermometer. Let the other end of the tube hang into the cup of water under the bulb. This is the wet-bulb thermometer. The other is the dry-bulb thermometer.

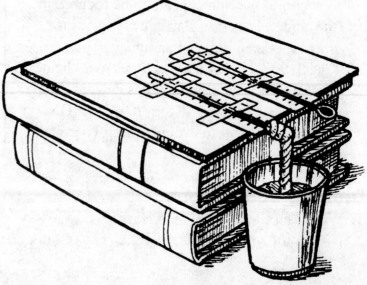

4. Fan the bulbs with the other piece of cardboard. Wait until the wet-bulb temperature stays the same for a minute. Record the wet-bulb and dry-bulb temperatures.

5. Subtract the smaller number from the larger one to find the difference between the two temperatures.

6. Use the chart on the next page to find relative humidity. First, on the left-hand side of the chart, find the row for the dry-bulb temperature. Then, at the top of the chart, find the column for the difference between the two temperatures. The number where the row and column meet is the relative humidity.

Can You Record Changes in Humidity?, page 2

Dry-bulb Temp. (°C)	Difference between wet-bulb and dry-bulb temperatures (°C)																	
	1°	2°	3°	4°	5°	6°	7°	8°	9°	10°	11°	12°	13°	14°	15°	16°	17°	18°
11°	89	78	67	56	46	36	27	18	9									
12°	89	78	68	58	48	39	29	21	12									
13°	89	79	69	59	50	41	32	23	15	7								
14°	90	79	70	60	51	42	34	26	18	10								
15°	90	80	71	61	53	44	36	27	20	13	6							
16°	90	81	71	63	54	46	38	30	23	15	8							
17°	90	81	72	64	55	47	40	32	25	18	11							
18°	91	82	73	65	57	49	41	34	27	20	14	7						
19°	91	82	74	65	58	50	43	36	29	22	16	10						
20°	91	83	74	66	59	51	44	37	31	24	18	12	6					
21°	91	83	75	67	60	53	46	39	32	26	20	14	9					
22°	92	83	76	68	61	54	47	40	34	28	22	17	11	6				
23°	92	84	76	69	62	55	48	42	36	30	24	19	13	8				
24°	92	84	77	69	62	56	49	43	37	31	26	20	15	10	5			
25°	92	84	77	70	63	57	50	44	39	33	28	22	17	12	8			
26°	92	85	78	71	64	58	51	46	40	34	29	24	19	14	10	5		
27°	92	85	78	71	65	58	52	47	41	36	31	26	21	16	12	7		
28°	93	85	78	72	65	59	53	48	42	37	32	27	22	18	13	9	5	
29°	93	86	79	72	66	60	54	49	43	38	33	28	24	19	15	11	7	
30°	93	86	79	73	67	61	55	50	44	39	35	30	25	21	17	13	9	5

Drawing Conclusions

1. What relative humidity reading did you get?
2. Predict how your classroom's relative humidity compares with the relative humidity outside. Test your prediction. How accurate was it?
3. Predict how your readings would be different outside on a rainy day. Test your prediction. How accurate was it?

MORE IDEAS

1. Include the chart in your display.
2. Keep a record of the humidity each day for a week. Get the weather report showing the humidity for each of those days. You can get a weather report in the newspaper or on the TV. How accurate is your psychrometer?
3. Do research to find out how humidity is related to different kinds of weather.

Name _____   Date _____

Can You Make a Compass?

Scientists believe that the Earth's interior acts something like a bar
magnet. This gives the Earth its north and south magnetic poles. A
magnetic field originates at the poles and surrounds the Earth. This
magnetic field has been detected by astronauts in space. They floated
magnets in their space capsules and found that the magnets moved to
stay in line with the Earth's magnetic field. On the Earth, a compass with a magnetized
needle also lines up with the Earth's magnetic field. Here's how to make a compass.

MATERIALS

a clear plastic cup no larger than 6 cm on the bottom
a sewing needle
a large index card
a strong magnet
a real compass
paste

Procedure

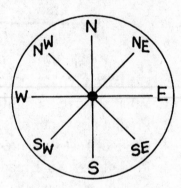

1. Cut out the compass circle
   and paste it to the index card.
2. To make the needle a
   magnet, place the needle on
   the magnet. Leave it there for
   30 minutes. Remove the
   needle from the magnet by
   lifting it straight up.
3. Fill the cup with water, and carefully lay the magnetized needle on the surface of the
   water. Be sure there is no metal nearby. Turn the cup until the needle points to north on
   the compass circle. Paste the cup to the circle.
4. Use the real compass to check your homemade compass. How accurate is your compass?

Drawing Conclusions

1. Does your compass point north? How do you know?
2. Would this compass work on the Moon? Why or why not?

How Does the Moon Revolve Around the Earth?

The Moon is the Earth's nearest neighbor in space. You can make a model to show how the Moon revolves around the Earth.

MATERIALS

a table-tennis ball   2 pieces of string
a tennis ball   a plastic drinking straw

Procedure

1. Tie one string tightly around the tennis ball. Pass one end of the string through the plastic straw. Then, tie the other end tightly around the table-tennis ball.
2. Find the balance point of the straw. Then, hang the straw and balls from the other string.
3. Wind up the system by turning the table-tennis ball around the string. Turn the ball around about 20 times.
4. Allow the string to unwind. As it does, watch the motion of the two balls.

Drawing Conclusions

1. Where is the place around which the tennis ball (Earth) revolved?
2. Where is the place around which the table-tennis ball (Moon) revolved?
3. Did the tennis and table-tennis balls revolve around the same point?

MORE IDEAS

1. Include your model with your display. Demonstrate the model for the judges.
2. Do people on the Earth see only one side of the Moon? Do research to find out.
3. What problems did the *Apollo* astronauts have landing on the Moon? Do research to find out.

How Do the Stars Look from Space?

Year after year, the constellations stay the same. The patterns you see among the stars at night do not change. Would they look different if you traveled into space? To find out, try this.

MATERIALS

large cardboard box	tape	flashlight
popped popcorn	needle	black thread
black construction paper	chalk	scissors

Procedure

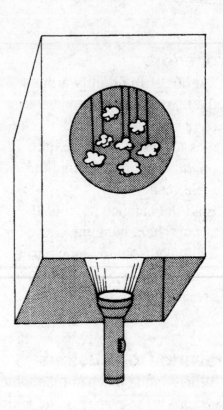

1. Tape black construction paper to the inside of the box.
2. With scissors, cut a round hole on each side of the box. Cover each hole with a flap of black construction paper taped to the outside. Number the holes. The inside of the box represents outer space.
3. Cut a piece of black thread 15 cm long. Thread the needle, and knot the thread at one end. Pull one piece of popcorn along the thread and down to the knot. Remove the thread from the needle.
4. Repeat with six more pieces of popcorn and with threads of different lengths. The popcorn represents the stars.
5. Tape the threads to the inside of the box. Then, turn the box upside down. Make sure that each piece of popcorn hangs freely.
6. Turn on the flashlight. Place it under the box, and look through one of the viewing holes.

Drawing Conclusions

1. What can you call the pattern of stars that you see?
2. Does the pattern look the same from every viewing hole? Why or why not?

MORE IDEAS

1. Do research on the Hubble Space Telescope. Does it offer a different view of space than Earth-based telescopes do?
2. Look through each viewing hole. Draw the pattern you see through each hole, using chalk and black construction paper.

Life Science Project

A science fair project can help you to understand the world around you better. Choose a topic that interests you. Then, use the Scientific Method to develop your project. Here's an example:

1. **PROBLEM:** How do plants react to major changes in their environment?

2. **HYPOTHESIS:** Plants do not thrive when major changes occur in their environments.

3. **EXPERIMENTATION:** Materials: 6 small houseplants, such as geraniums, labels. Label each of the six pots **A** through **F**. Keep one plant moist and in the sunlight. This will be the control plant. Keep one plant very wet; keep another very dry. Give one plant no sunlight and another plant no air. Put one plant in the refrigerator. Keep a record of how the plants respond each day for one week.

4. **OBSERVATION:** The only plant that is thriving is the control plant. The others are turning yellow or brown, rotting, or wilting.

5. **CONCLUSION:** Plants do not thrive when there are major changes to their environments.

6. **COMPARISON:** The conclusion and the hypothesis agree.

7. **PRESENTATION:** Include all the plants in your presentation. Display your records and explain what was done to each plant. You may want to take photographs of your plants as the week goes by to use in your presentation.

8. **RESOURCES:** Tell of any reading you did to help you with your experiment. Tell who helped you get materials and set up the experiment.

MORE ✎ **IDEAS**

1. How does air pollution affect plants?
2. What kinds of farming methods can preserve the nutrients in soil?
3. What would happen to the biosphere if the Earth lost its atmosphere?
4. How does imprinting help young animals to survive?
5. What is the difference between instinctual and learned behavior?
6. Can a lack of certain food groups or nutrients affect the way people look or feel?
7. How can regional diets affect the appearance of a population?
8. Can a person prevent reflexive movement?

How Do You Know If a Food Contains Starch?

Starch is an important part of many foods. It is a carbohydrate and an important part of our diet. Some people, though, must limit the amount of starch they eat. Here is one way to find out if a food contains starch.

MATERIALS

bread	apple slice	wax paper
cooked rice	bologna	eyedropper
raw potato	butter	iodine

CAUTION: Iodine is a poison. It should never be tasted.

Procedure

1. Put a small piece of each food on a piece of wax paper. (You may use the same piece of wax paper to hold all the foods.)
2. Use the eyedropper to place three drops of iodine on each piece of food.
3. If a black spot appears on the food, it contains starch.
4. Make a list of all the foods that contain starch.

Drawing Conclusions

1. Do any of the foods change color?
2. What happens to the foods that contain starch?

 MORE IDEAS

1. Include your setup and findings in your display. Demonstrate your test for the judges.
2. Research to find other foods that contain starch. Include a list in your report.
3. How important is starch in your diet? What diseases or medical problems might cause you to limit your starch intake?

Name _____   Date _____

How Good Is Your Sense of Taste?

The sense of taste allows us to identify foods and to enjoy their flavor. But just how good is your sense of taste? Work with partners to find out. Have separate toothpicks, water, and food samples for each person tested.

MATERIALS

blindfold
toothpicks
paper cup of water
5 food samples

You may wish to use 10 different foods and keep the cups covered so that the tasters do not see the foods before they taste them.

Procedure

1. Blindfold the taster.
2. Give the taster five food samples, each in a numbered cup.
3. Using a toothpick, pick up a small amount of one food sample. Tell the taster to hold his or her nose. Then, place the food on the taster's tongue.

4. Tell the taster to roll the sample around on his or her tongue. Then, ask the taster to identify the type of taste (sweet, bitter, salty, etc.) and to name the food. Record the response in your chart.
5. Repeat steps 3 and 4 with each food sample. Have the taster drink some water after each sample to clear the taste buds. Use a new toothpick each time.
6. Continue to test other people. Record the results.

Sample	Taste described as...	Food identified as...

Drawing Conclusions

1. Which food samples did each taster guess correctly?
2. Were there any food samples that the tasters could not identify?
3. Why might a taster have difficulty identifying some of the foods?
4. Would the results be the same if the tasters could see the food? Why or why not?
5. Would the results be the same if the tasters did not hold their noses? Why or why not?

Name _____   Date _____

How Can You Change Your Pulse Rate?

Your pulse rate does not stay the same all the time. You can find out how it is changed by standing up, lying down, and exercising.

MATERIALS

a clock or a watch with a second hand

Procedure

1. Stand up for two minutes. While standing, hold your fingers in the correct position for feeling your pulse. Ask a helper to signal the beginning and end of one minute. Find your pulse rate. Record it in the chart.
2. Lie down for two minutes. Then, take your pulse rate, and record it in the chart.
3. Sit up for two minutes. At the end of two minutes, take your pulse rate. Record it in the chart.
4. Run in place for one minute. As soon as you stop, take your pulse rate. Record it in the chart.

Situation	Pulse rate
Standing	
Lying down	
Sitting	
After running	

Drawing Conclusions

1. When was your pulse rate the slowest?
2. When was your pulse rate the fastest?
3. Why does your pulse rate speed up when you exercise?

MORE ✓ IDEAS

1. Try other activities to see how they affect your pulse rate, such as jumping rope or holding your breath for one minute.
2. Do research on pulse rates. What rates are considered normal for people of different ages?

Name _____ Date _____

What Is Your Lung Capacity?

How much air can you inhale or exhale in one breath? Do this activity to find out how much air your lungs hold.

MATERIALS

two 2-liter plastic soda bottles
two rubber tubes or flexible drinking straws
a large measuring cup or graduated cylinder

a plastic dishpan
cardboard
water

Procedure

1. Place a strip of tape on the outside of each bottle, from top to bottom.
2. Pour 100 mL of water into the bottle. Then, draw a line on the tape to mark the water level. Repeat this step until the bottle is full of water. Label the lines 100 mL, 200 mL, 300 mL, and so on. Do the same thing for the second bottle.
3. Pour water into the dishpan to a depth of 5 cm. Fill the two soda bottles with water, and cover the openings with cardboard. Invert the bottles in the tub of water. Remove the covers, being careful not to let any air into the bottles.
4. Insert the short end of a soda straw or rubber tube into each bottle. Take a deep breath. Then, exhale completely through the straw or tube into the bottle. The air should replace the water in the bottle. When you fill the bottle, switch to the second bottle.

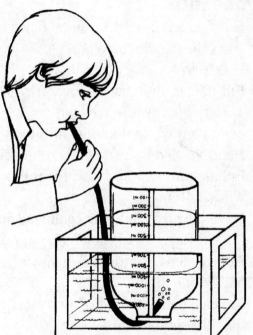

5. Observe the water level in the bottles. How does this activity measure the air in your lungs? As you breathed out, the air pushed the water out of the jug. The amount of water you push out is the same as the amount of air you breathe out.

Drawing Conclusions

1. How much air did you exhale?
2. Let other people do the activity. What is the average amount of air exhaled by the people tested?

Unit 2: Life Science
Science Projects 5–6, SV 6911-6

Name _____ Date _____

Does Holding Your Breath Change the Amounts of Oxygen and Carbon Dioxide You Exhale?

MATERIALS

1-qt. glass jar	clear plastic box
water	flexible drinking straw
cardboard	clock or watch with second hand
candle in candlestick	

Procedure

1. Have an adult light a candle. Place a jar over it. Record the time it takes the candle to go out.
2. Pour 6 to 8 cm of water into the plastic box.
3. Fill the jar with water. Cover it with cardboard.
4. Turn the jar over in the water of the plastic box. Remove the cardboard without letting air into the jar.
5. Bend the end of a straw. Put it under the rim of the jar.
6. Exhale through the straw, forcing the water out until there is no water left in the jar.
7. Have the adult light the candle again. Quickly, cover the candle with the jar. Record how much time it takes for the candle to go out.
8. Repeat steps 2 through 7. This time, hold your breath for 10 seconds before exhaling.
9. Repeat steps 2 through 7 two more times. Each time, hold your breath 10 seconds longer than the time before.

Drawing Conclusions

1. Why did the candle go out?
2. How did the length of time the candle burned compare with the length of time you held your breath?
3. How does holding your breath change the amount of carbon dioxide you exhale? Explain.

How Far Apart Are Nerve Cells?

Your skin, along with your hair and nails, makes up the integumentary system. This system provides a protective layer for your body. Your skin contains nerve cells, or neurons, that give you your sense of touch. Do all areas of your skin have the same number of nerve cells? Can you feel things as well on every part of your body?

MATERIALS

scarf
two toothpicks
ruler

Procedure

1. With the scarf, blindfold a helper. Hold the two toothpicks together, and poke the helper gently on the fingertip until he or she can feel the pressure. It should feel as if there is only one toothpick. Then, move the toothpicks slightly apart and try it again. How many toothpicks did your helper feel?

2. Keep moving the toothpicks apart until your helper feels the touch of two toothpicks.

3. Measure the distance between the toothpicks. This measurement is the distance between two nerve cells. Record the number in the chart.

4. Repeat the activity on the back of the hand, the cheek, and the back of the neck. Record your measurements in the chart.

Location	Distance between toothpicks
Fingertip	
Back of hand	
Cheek	
Back of neck	

Drawing Conclusions

1. Where are the nerve cells farthest apart? Why do you think they are so far apart at that part of the body?

2. Where are the nerve cells closest together? Why do you think they are so close?

MORE IDEAS

1. Perform the activity for the judges. Try to get a judge to volunteer to be the helper.

2. Draw a "map" of the nerve cells at different places on the body. Include your map with your display.

Name _____ Date _____

How Does Skin Protect
Against Infection?

Bright and shiny apples—red, green, and yellow. The "skin" of an apple is more than just something colorful to look at. Find out how skin is helpful by doing this activity.

MATERIALS

two small paper plates   crayon or marking pen
two fresh apples   plastic knife
one rotten apple

Procedure

1. Label one of the paper plates **uncut skin**. Label the other one **cut skin**.
2. Place a fresh apple on each paper plate.
3. Cut a badly spoiled piece off the rotten apple.
4. Cut a piece of skin off the apple labeled **cut skin**. Rub the piece of rotten apple on the area where the skin was removed. Some of the rotten apple should stick to the fresh apple.
5. Next, rub the same piece of the rotten apple on the apple labeled **uncut skin**.
6. Discard the rotten apple and the cuttings. Clean up your area, and wash your hands.
7. Put the paper plates with the apples aside. Observe the cut and the uncut apples each day for one week. Record your observations in the chart.

Observations

Day	Apple with cut skin	Apple with uncut skin
1		
2		
3		
4		
5		
6		
7		

Drawing Conclusions

1. Describe what happened to the cut and uncut apples. How can you explain the difference in the two apples?
2. How is your skin like the skin of an apple?

How Good Is Your Short-Term Memory?

People use their memories for many things. Sometimes, they remember things that happened long ago. Other times, they must remember things that just happened. This second kind of remembering is called short-term memory. How good is your short-term memory? Do this activity to find out.

MATERIALS

15 assorted items such as a cup, fork, pair of glasses, book, picture in frame, hammer, sock, shoe, clock, apple, banana, small radio

a box that will fit over the items

clock or watch with second hand

Procedure

1. Place 10 of the items on a table, and set the box over them.
2. Find a volunteer. Tell the person to try to remember all the items you will show in Step 3.
3. Remove the box. Give the person 30 seconds to look at the items. Cover them again with the box.
4. Ask the volunteer to list the things he or she remembers. How many did the person remember? Record the number in the chart.
5. Repeat the procedure three more times. Each time, switch some of the items.
6. Test several people. After each person is tested, make a chart to show the results.

Trial	Number of objects remembered
1	
2	
3	
4	

Drawing Conclusions

1. Did the volunteers tested remember more things each time?
2. Why do you think their memories improved or got worse?

MORE IDEAS

1. Mount photos on poster board. Show them to a volunteer for 30 seconds. Then, set the photos aside. Ask the person to describe the photos he or she remembers. Make a chart that shows which photos were most remembered, which photos were least remembered, which photos males remembered most, and which photos females remembered most.
2. What do you conclude from the information in your chart? Write a paragraph explaining your conclusions.

Can Inherited Traits Be Affected by the Environment?

We inherit traits from our parents. Is it possible that some of these inherited traits are affected by our surroundings? Try this experiment to find out about the inherited traits of marigolds.

MATERIALS

small stones	two saucers
two flowerpots	water
potting soil	sand
package of tall marigold seeds	

Procedure

1. Place the small stones in the bottoms of the two flowerpots.
2. Fill one pot with sand to 1 cm from the top.
3. Fill the other pot with soil to 1 cm from the top.
4. Plant four marigold seeds in each pot. Read the package to find out how deep the seeds should be planted.
5. Place each pot on a saucer. Water the seeds.
6. Put the pots on a sunny windowsill. Each pot should get the same amount of sunlight every day. Keep the soil moist.
7. Complete the chart as the plants grow.

Seed traits	Seeds in sand	Seeds in soil
Days taken to sprout		
Height when grown		

Drawing Conclusions

1. Did the seeds sprout at about the same time?
2. In which pot were the marigolds taller?
3. In which pot did the marigolds look healthier?
4. What inherited trait was affected by the environment?
5. What differences between the soil and the sand may have affected the plants' growth?
6. What other variables might affect plant growth?

Name _____ Date _____

Can You Select Traits to Pass On?

Creatures gain their traits from their parents. Is it possible that certain traits can be emphasized so they are passed from generation to generation? Try this experiment to find out.

MATERIALS

a banana   two small jars
cotton   magnifying glass
white plate   an artist's brush
                        paper towel

Procedure

1. Put a piece of banana in the bottom of a jar. Put a strip of loosely folded paper towel over the banana. Leave the jar uncapped for two to three days. When you see several small flies in the jar, put the cap on.

2. Observe the fruit flies with the magnifying glass. Look for differences in the shape of wings or the color of eyes. Males are smaller, and the tips of their abdomens are darker-colored.

3. Put the jar and the white plate in the refrigerator. Then, prepare another small jar with some banana and a cotton plug for the opening.

4. Take the cold flies from the refrigerator. Quickly spill them on the cold plate. With an artist's brush, select several with one trait difference that you would like to crossbreed. Put them in the fresh jar, and insert the plug. Wait for the next generation.

Drawing Conclusions

1. What differences did you find among the flies?
2. What characteristics did you select to crossbreed?
3. What happened to those characteristics in the second generation?
4. Which was the dominant trait?
5. Why should you select flies with only one difference?

MORE IDEAS

1. Include your setup and results with your display.
2. Continue the experiment for several more generations. How successful are you in selecting traits to pass on?

Name _____   Date _____

How Does a Caterpillar Metamorphose?

You have probably studied the metamorphosis of some insects. You know that the caterpillar changes into a butterfly. In this activity, you will observe the changes a caterpillar undergoes.

MATERIALS

a large glass jar with a lid
a plastic bag
fresh leaves and twigs

CAUTION: An adult should help you punch holes in the lid of the jar.

Procedure

1. Find a caterpillar eating a leaf. Place it into a plastic bag along with some leaves and twigs from the plant.
2. Carefully place the contents of the plastic bag into the jar.
3. Observe how the caterpillar moves and eats. If possible, watch it spin its cocoon.
4. Keep a record of how long the caterpillar takes to spin its cocoon. Then, keep track of the time until it emerges from the cocoon. Include your observations in a chart.

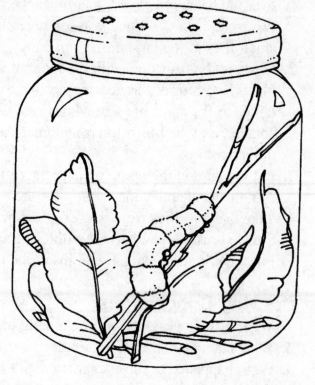

Drawing Conclusions

1. How many legs does the caterpillar have?
2. What is the cocoon made of?
3. What is happening when the caterpillar is inside its cocoon?
4. What kind of butterfly emerges from the cocoon?

MORE IDEAS

1. Try collecting caterpillars from different plants. Do different kinds of butterflies emerge?
2. Try feeding different foods to the same kind of caterpillars. Do changes in food affect the development or appearance of the butterfly?

How Do Some Animals Insulate Themselves from Heat?

Prairie dogs escape the heat of summer by going underground. See why they do this.

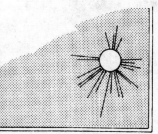

MATERIALS

two ice cubes that are the same size
pot of soil (or a folded towel)
two small plastic bags
two ties for plastic bags

Procedure

1. Put each ice cube in a bag, and tie the bag shut. Quickly bury one ice cube beneath the soil (or in the towel). Put the other ice cube on the top of the soil or towel.
2. Place your materials in a sunny window or under a lamp.
3. As soon as the top ice cube melts, dig out the other one.

Drawing Conclusions

1. Did the buried ice cube melt completely?
2. What protected it from the heat?

The soil above a prairie dog's tunnel provides insulation for the animal, just as it did for your ice cube. These tunnels are cool in summer and warm in winter, no matter what the temperature is outside.

MORE IDEAS

1. Do research to find how other animals protect themselves from the heat or cold. How do animals survive in the desert or in the polar areas?
2. Do research on underground homes. Why do people choose to build all or part of their home underground? What are the benefits?

Name _____ Date _____

Can You Make a Microscope?

Scientists use microscopes to study small objects like cells. A microscope magnifies an object so that it appears larger. You can make a small microscope to use at home or just about anywhere. Here's how.

MATERIALS

water   newspaper or magazine
small nail   aluminum pie pan
cotton swab

Procedure

1. Put a thick newspaper or magazine under the pie pan to protect the table top. Carefully push the nail slowly and firmly into the bottom of the pie pan until it makes a small, round hole.

2. Wet the cotton swab with water. Carefully let a drop of water fall from the swab into the hole. The drop should remain in the hole, not drip down through it. If the hole is too big, make a smaller hole in another spot and try again.

3. Choose an object to look at through your microscope. A piece of newspaper with small print, a patterned scarf, or a coin should work well. Hold the pan just above the object. Look at the object through the water drop. Look at several other objects. How do they look?

You have made a water-drop microscope.
The drop of water acts like one of the lenses of an actual microscope.

MORE IDEAS

1. Include your microscope with your display. Demonstrate the microscope for the judges.
2. Research some of the early microscopes, such as the one used by Robert Hooke. Include your findings in your report.
3. Research the electron microscope. Include your findings in your report.

Name _____ Date _____

Are You a Scientist?

You have probably studied the parts of a cell. Robert Hooke was a famous scientist who learned about cells by looking at a thin slice of cork under his microscope. See what you can learn by looking at the same thing!

MATERIALS

very thin slice of cork   leaves
microscope slides   microscope
dropper bottle of water

Procedure

1. Place a very thin slice of cork in a drop of water on a microscope slide.
2. Place the slide under the microscope, and adjust the focus.
3. Draw what you see. Label the cells that Robert Hooke viewed.
4. Break off a small piece of a leaf, and put it in a drop of water on a microscope slide.
5. Place the slide under the microscope, and adjust the focus.
6. Draw and label what you see this time.
7. Try looking at other things under the microscope. Remember always to use a very thin piece of whatever you are looking at. Draw and label what you see. Can you see cells? If you can, label the parts.

Drawing Conclusions

1. Did you find cells in everything you observed? Explain.
2. How are the cells of the different plants alike? How are the cells different?

Name _____ Date _____

What Can You Observe in Onion Skin Cells?

You have probably studied the parts of a plant cell. In this activity, you will be able to see these parts in a thin piece of onion skin containing cells.

MATERIALS

piece of onion	eyedropper
a microscope slide	iodine
forceps (tweezers)	microscope
a cover slip	

CAUTION: Iodine is a poison. Be careful when using it.

Procedure

1. Soak the onion slice in water for a few minutes. Use the forceps to gently separate the layers of the onion. Pull apart a small section that is about the size of your fingernail.
2. Place a drop of water on the slide, and put the piece of onion skin on it. Place the cover slip on the onion skin.
3. Place the slide on the microscope. Move the barrel of the microscope up until you get the cells in focus. You may need to move the slide around to find the thinnest part of the onion skin. Make a drawing in the box below of what you see under the microscope.
4. Some structures of cells are hard to see even using a microscope. To make them visible, scientists sometimes add something that stains the cells. You can stain your onion cells by putting a drop of iodine on the onion skin slide. Describe what you observed after you stained the onion skin.

Drawing Conclusions

1. What are the parts of a plant cell?
2. Are cells easier to see when they have been stained?

Name _____   Date _____

What Do Some Kinds of Protists Look Like?

Protists are tiny one-celled organisms that show some characteristics of both plants and animals. This activity shows you what some protists look like.

MATERIALS

jar of pond water   microscope
cover slips   microscope slides
eyedropper

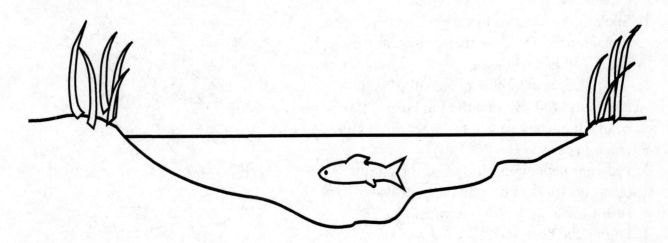

Procedure

1. Put a drop of pond water on a microscope slide. Place a cover slip over the drop of water.
2. Put the slide on the microscope stage.
3. Lower the bottom lens until it nearly touches the slide. Look through the microscope.
4. Raise the lens slowly until you can see clearly into the drop of water. CAUTION: Do not lower the lens while you look through the microscope. You might break the slide or lens.
5. Look for protists swimming in the water. Move the slide around gently; don't lift it.
6. Draw the protists that you see. Label any parts of cells that you can identify.

Drawing Conclusions

1. How many different kinds of protists did you see? Can you identify any of them?
2. How would you describe the shape of the protists you saw?
3. How did the protists move?
4. What can you conclude about the colors, sizes, shapes, and structures of protists?

Why Do Living Things Need Food?

You need to eat every day. Food gives you energy. It also provides the materials you need to grow and to repair body tissue. Plants need food for the same reasons. You can see how a bean seed uses some of its stored food in this activity.

MATERIALS

four bean seeds	water
aluminum foil	soil
paper cup (plastic-coated)	

Procedure

1. Soak the bean seeds in water overnight. Then look at them. Describe them. How do they feel when you handle them?
2. Wrap one bean tightly in a small piece of aluminum foil. Be sure the foil covers the bean completely so that no water or air can reach it.
3. Fill your paper cup $\frac{3}{4}$ full of soil. Plant the beans about 3 cm deep in the soil. Water the soil. Keep it moist for one week.
4. Dig up the bean seeds.

Drawing Conclusions

1. How do the unwrapped beans look? How do they feel? What other changes have occurred? Where did the food come from for these changes?
2. Unwrap the bean in aluminum foil. How is it different from the other beans?

Under the right conditions, a bean seed will use its stored food to grow a new plant. If the bean has no oxygen or water, however, it cannot use the stored food.

Name _____ Date _____

How Are Fruit Seeds Alike and Different?

For people, fruits such as apples and tomatoes are tasty foods. For flowering plants, fruits are seed holders. Fruits contain the seeds that will grow into new plants.

As you know, seed types vary greatly. Apple seeds are small and tear-shaped. The whole coconut fruit is a seed—and it's huge. Some fruits, such as the watermelon, have many seeds. Others, like the mango, contain just one. Seeds can be soft, like those of cucumbers, or they can be hard, like the seed of a plum. In the following activity, you'll take a close look at seeds and compare them.

MATERIALS

various kinds of fruit
knife
pencil
chart

CAUTION: Be careful using the knife.

Procedure

1. Slice a fruit in half.
2. Gather the information about the fruit to fill in the chart.
3. Repeat the procedure to complete the chart for all the fruits you are studying.

Fruit Seeds

Fruit	Number of seeds	Seed size	Seed color	Seed shape	Seed hardness

Drawing Conclusions

1. Describe the characteristics of each seed that would help it survive and grow.
2. Some fruits have more seeds than others. What advantage might that give them?

Name _____ Date _____

What Are Tropisms?

A seed sprouts. A tiny stem and roots grow from it. The stem pokes up through the soil and grows toward the sky. The roots grow deeper into the soil. How does this happen? Why do stems always grow up and roots always grow down?

Plant reactions called *tropisms* are part of the answer. These reactions to environmental conditions cause parts of plants to grow in certain ways.

Geotropism is a plant root's tendency to grow downward with the force of gravity. Phototropism is a plant stem's tendency to grow toward the light. You may have seen a plant on a windowsill grow toward the Sun. To find out about phototropism, try this experiment. Set the pots up and label them as shown below.

MATERIALS

three plants of the same type and size
chart

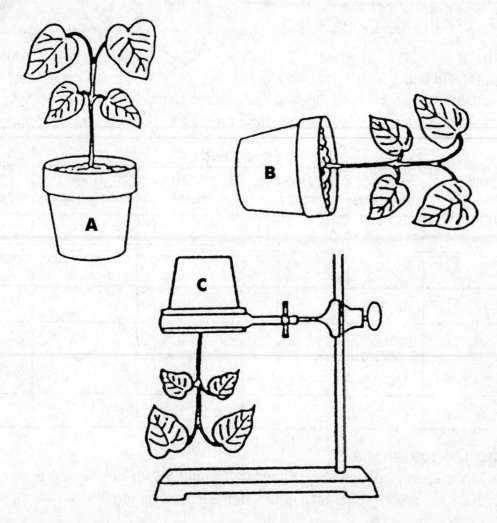

What Are Tropisms?, page 2

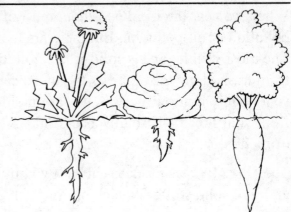

Procedure

1. Observe the stems of the three plants at the start of the experiment. In the boxes of the chart, draw the way the plants look.
2. Observe the stems of the plants over a three-week period. Record what you see each week.

Plant Stem Growth

Drawing	Plant A	Plant B	Plant C
Direction of stem growth at the start of the experiment			
Direction of stem growth after one week			
Direction of stem growth after two weeks			
Direction of stem growth after three weeks			

Drawing Conclusions

1. What caused the plant stems to grow as they did?
2. Infer how the plant stems would have grown if the plants had been placed on a glass table with a light source under the table.
3. Which way do you think the roots of each plant in the experiment would be growing after three weeks?

MORE IDEAS

1. Include your setup and findings in your display.
2. Think of other ways that you can manipulate the growth of the plants.

Do You Pollute?

When we hear the word *pollution*, most of us think of either water pollution or air pollution. But there are many other types of pollution. The most visible type is solid-waste pollution. This includes anything from trash along the highway to junked cars and old tires. Anything solid that you throw away—such as an old comic book or the leftovers from your lunch—is solid waste. And any waste that harms the environment is a form of pollution.

The United States produces about two billion tons of solid waste each year. That's about 20 kg of solid waste for each person each day! Think about how much waste that is—about half your body mass.

What can we do about solid waste? The good news is that with a little effort, we can cut down on pollution. We can recycle.

Think about an aluminum can. You can throw it away, or you can recycle it. When you throw it away, it will probably be taken with the rest of your garbage to a landfill. The smell of a landfill pollutes the air. In some cases, materials in the landfill leak down through the soil and pollute underground water.

Think a little more about the aluminum can. If you recycle it, you won't be adding it to an overfilled landfill. But just as important as that, reusing aluminum means saving natural resources and saving energy. Any aluminum that is recycled will not need to be mined from the ground. Energy that would be needed to process new aluminum ore will be saved.

In the last few years, many communities have started recycling aluminum cans, glass bottles and jars, and newspapers. Some communities have also begun to recycle other waste, such as tin-covered steel cans and plastic containers. Each item that is recycled saves energy and doesn't add to solid-waste pollution. You can help. Find out how much you and your family can recycle.

MATERIALS

paper grocery bags
marking pen
trash

Name _____   Date _____

Do You Pollute?, page 2

Procedure

1. Keep track of all the things you can recycle in one week. Before you throw something away, think about whether it could be recycled.
2. Organize your recycling. Label a paper grocery bag for each type of item that can be recycled. You should have one bag for each of the following: newspapers; magazines and junk mail; cardboard; glass; aluminum; and tin.
3. Ask your family to help by putting anything that can be recycled into the right bag.
4. At the end of the week, fill out the following table to find out how much you recycled. For the paper and cardboard recycling, you can weigh each type if you have a scale. Otherwise, count the number of newspapers, magazines, and cardboard boxes. Count the number of cans and bottles in each category.
5. Most communities recycle some things. Find out whether your community will accept the items you separated for recycling.

Recycling for the Week of _____ **to** _____

Newspaper	Cardboard	Magazines and junk mail	Glass	Aluminum	Tin

Drawing Conclusions

1. If recycling is so helpful, why do you think many people do not recycle?
2. What can you do to help prevent solid-waste pollution?
3. Do research on recycling during World War II. Why were people in the United States then more willing to recycle? Include your findings in your report.

What Are Decomposers?

Along with plants and animals, decomposers are important to the balance of nature. The decomposers, such as mold and bacteria, break down dead organisms and waste and return them to the soil. Plants then use the soil to grow. This completes the cycle. Where can you find decomposers? What do they need in order to be active? To find out, try this activity.

MATERIALS

marking pen	four plastic containers
newspaper	sand
potting soil	water

Procedure

1. Label the four containers **dry soil**, **damp soil**, **dry sand**, and **damp sand**.
2. Tear four strips of newspaper about 4 cm wide and 12 cm long. Lay each strip in a plastic container, with one end of the strip hanging over the edge.
3. Fill the two containers labeled **dry soil** and **damp soil** with potting soil. Fill the other two containers with clean sand. One end of the strip of newspaper should stick out of the soil or sand in each container.
4. Add a little water to the containers labeled **damp soil** and **damp sand**. Add water to the containers every few days to keep the soil and sand damp.
5. Observe the condition of the strips of newspaper in the containers for one week. Record your observations in the chart.

Day	Dry soil	Damp soil	Dry sand	Damp sand
1				
2				
3				
4				
5				
6				
7				

What Are Decomposers?, page 2

Drawing Conclusions

1. In which container did the strip of newspaper decompose the most? Explain why you think this happened.
2. What happened to the strip of newspaper in the containers that were kept dry? Explain why you think this happened.
3. What could account for the difference in decomposition in the container with the damp soil and the one with the damp sand?
4. How do decomposers help the environment?

MORE IDEAS

1. Include your setup and findings in your display.
2. Add arrows to the diagram below to show how energy flows through a food web. Include the diagram in your display.

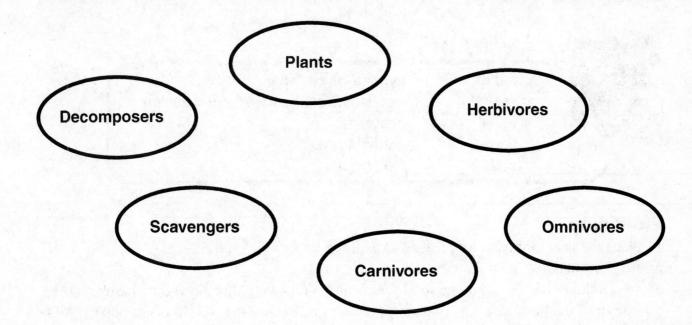

Does Composting Really Work?

When your family finishes dinner, you can recycle the jars, bottles, and boxes the food came in. If you have leftover food, you can recycle that, too. Food is organic waste. It is made of things that were once living, like animals and plants. Organic garbage includes food wastes and leaves and grass from lawns. Paper and wood are organic waste, too, since they were once trees.

As much as half the garbage you throw out may be organic, and you can recycle it as compost. Composting means turning organic garbage into natural fertilizer. To make compost from garbage, you mix the garbage with soil and worms. The worms and the bacteria in the compost break down the garbage into rich material loaded with minerals. The compost can be added to soil and used to grow plants.

Compost is useful in another way, too. The garbage you turn into compost doesn't have to be thrown into garbage dumps. Most garbage dumps have very little space left. You can make compost on a small scale, but be patient. It will take a few months before it is ready to use. Here's what you do.

MATERIALS

red worms	torn leaves or paper
soil	wooden box (70 cm x 70 cm x 20 cm)
water	peat moss
bowl	garden trowel
scale	food scraps

Procedure

1. Place the peat moss and torn leaves or paper in the box.
2. Add two handfuls of soil.
3. Weigh the bowl. Then, put the food scraps into it and weigh the bowl again. Subtract the weight of the bowl to get the weight of the scraps. Record the weight of the scraps. Add the food scraps to the box.
4. Add 500 g of worms to the box for every 250 g of scraps.
5. Mix the compost with a trowel. Sprinkle it with water to make it damp, but not soggy.
6. Leave your compost bin in the sunlight. Turn the compost, and sprinkle it with water every few days. Your compost will take several months to form. Then, use it for planting.

Drawing Conclusions

1. Make a list of everything you throw away in one day. How much could be composted?
2. What are the advantages of making and using compost?

Name _____   Date _____

Physical Science Project

A science fair project can help you to understand the world around you better. Choose a topic that interests you. Then, use the Scientific Method to develop your project. Here's an example:

1. **PROBLEM:** Is the dye of a felt-tip marker a compound?
2. **HYPOTHESIS:** The dye in a felt-tip marker is a compound because the dye is made from a blend of colors.
3. **EXPERIMENTATION:** Materials: felt-tip markers, coffee filters, small jars, water, scissors
   Cut several filters so they have a 10-cm diameter. Cut two lines of radius 1 cm apart to make a tail on each filter. Fill the jars with water. Set a filter on each jar, with the tail pushed into the water. Make a chart that shows your observations.
4. **OBSERVATION:** Blue dye filters out to be yellow and green.
5. **CONCLUSION:** Dyes are compounds because they can be separated.
6. **COMPARISON:** The conclusion and the hypothesis agree.
7. **PRESENTATION:** Set up the experiment for others to duplicate. Show your chart.
8. **RESOURCES:** Name the books you used. Tell who helped you get the materials and set up the experiment.

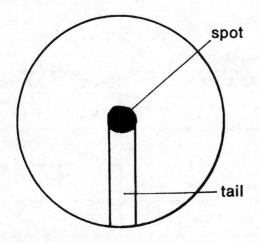
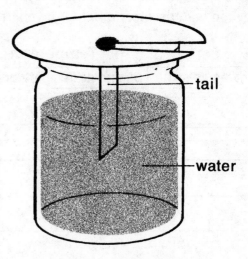

MORE IDEAS

1. What metals could you use to build a tree house outside? Which metals would rust the least? Collect nails, screws, and bolts made out of a variety of metals to find out.
2. What chemical reaction takes place in gasoline to make a car's engine run? Do research to find out.
3. Make a model of one of the elements on the periodic table. Which materials does it react with to make different compounds?

Name _____ Date _____

How Can You Reduce Heat Loss?

To conserve energy, most people insulate their homes. How does insulation work? Try this experiment to find out.

MATERIALS

hot water	baby food jar
shoe box	a variety of insulating materials
clock	thermometer

Procedure

1. Put the hot water in a baby food jar. Measure its temperature.
2. Pack the baby food jar in a shoe box filled with your choice of insulation.
3. Open the box after 45 minutes. Measure the temperature of the water.
4. Repeat Steps 1 through 3 with a different insulating material.
5. Record the kinds of insulation and the changes in water temperature on the chart.

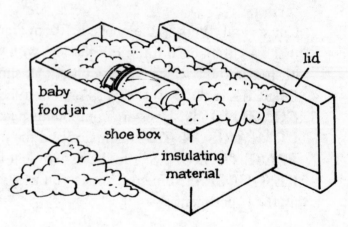

Temperature Measurement

Kind of Insulation	Beginning Temperature	Final Temperature	Change in Temperature

Drawing Conclusions

1. What kind of insulation worked best?
2. Is your home insulated? If so, what kind of insulation was used?

MORE IDEAS

1. Include your setup and chart in your display.
2. Do research to learn more about different insulating materials used in construction. Include details in your report.

Name _____   Date _____

How Do Crystals Form?

Crystals are particles that are arranged in an orderly pattern. Crystals come in all sizes. When liquid substances freeze, the temperature around them affects the size of the crystals formed. Try this experiment.

MATERIALS

magnifier	microscope slide
salt	2 small containers with lids
water	plastic stirrer
teaspoon	paper towel
dark paper	eyedropper

Procedure

1. Pour a teaspoon of salt into one container. Fill the container $\frac{3}{4}$ full of water. Stir the solution.
2. Lay a paper towel over the top of the second container. Push it slightly into the container to serve as a filter.
3. Pour the salt solution through the filter into the second container. Remove the filter.
4. Lay the slide on the dark paper. Place 2 or 3 drops of the salt solution on the slide.
5. Leave the slide for one day.
6. Use the magnifier to look at the slide.
7. Make a sketch of what you see.

Drawing Conclusions

1. Was there any water on the slide after one day?
2. What shape are the salt crystals?
3. Where did the salt crystals come from?
4. What caused salt crystals to form on the slide?

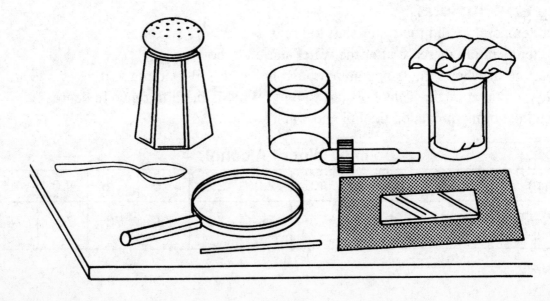

What Is the Boiling Point of a Liquid?

A physical change is one in which the molecules of a substance stay the same. The substance may look different, but its makeup is the same. Cutting and ripping are examples of physical changes. Melting and freezing a substance are also examples of physical changes.

MATERIALS

electric skillet	ruler	thermometer
cold water	goggles	stopwatch

CAUTION: This experiment must be done with an adult, and goggles must be worn.

Procedure

1. Fill the electric skillet with cold water to a depth of 3 cm.
2. Place the thermometer in the water.
3. Plug in the skillet and turn the power to high.
4. Record the temperature every 30 seconds for 4 minutes and 30 seconds.

Boiling Point of Water

Time (min)	0	0.5	1.0	1.5	2.0	2.5	3.0	3.5	4.0	4.5
Temperature of Water (°C)										

Drawing Conclusions

1. At what temperature did the water start to boil?
2. Did the temperature increase after the water started to boil?
3. The chart below shows the temperature of alcohol as it boils. Compare it to your chart. At which temperature does alcohol start to boil? What is the difference in degrees between the boiling points of alcohol and water?

Boiling Point of Alcohol

Time (min)	0	0.5	1.0	1.5	2.0	2.5	3.0	3.5	4.0	4.5
Temperature of Alcohol (°C)	20	45	77	78	78	78	78	78	78	78

Name _____   Date _____

Does the Amount of Matter Change After a Chemical Reaction?

When matter changes form in a chemical reaction, it looks, smells, and feels different. However, it still has the same mass.

MATERIALS

balloon	empty pill bottle
vinegar	small funnel
teaspoon	balance scale
baking soda	gram weights

Procedure

1. Pour 1 teaspoon of baking soda through the funnel into the balloon.
2. Fill the pill bottle half full with vinegar.
3. Pull the opening of the balloon over the mouth of the bottle.
4. Put the balloon and bottle on the balance scale. Add weights to the other side until the balance is level. Record the weight.
5. Remove the balloon and bottle from the scale. Pour the baking soda from the balloon into the pill bottle. Observe what happens.
6. Return the bottle and balloon to the scale. Again, weigh the materials and record the information.

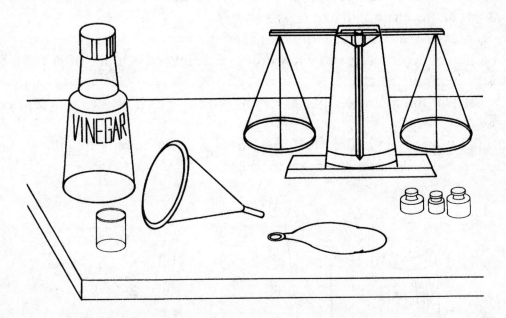

Drawing Conclusions

1. What happened when you mixed the baking soda and the vinegar in Step 5?
2. Did the balance scale remain level after returning the balloon and bottle to it in Step 6?
3. Was the amount of matter the same both before and after the chemical reaction? Explain.

How Can You Identify a Chemical Reaction?

A chemical reaction, or change, occurs when two or more substances are combined to make a new substance having new properties. Do this experiment to see a chemical reaction.

MATERIALS

teaspoon	cornstarch	aluminum foil
sugar	wax paper	baking soda
vinegar	matches	3 plastic cups
iodine	clothespin	2 eyedroppers
candle	goggles	permanent marker

CAUTION: This experiment must be done with an adult. Iodine is poisonous. Goggles must be worn.

Procedure

1. Label separate cups **A**, **B**, and **C**. Pour some baking soda into Cup A, sugar into Cup B, and cornstarch into Cup C.
2. Mark a sheet of wax paper with **A**, **B**, and **C**. Put 1 teaspoon of each powder on the wax paper next to the correct letter.
3. Using the eyedropper, add a few drops of vinegar to each pile of powder. Record your observations on the chart on the next page.
4. Repeat Step 2 using a clean sheet of wax paper.
5. Using a different eyedropper, add a few drops of iodine to each pile of powder. Record your observations on the chart.
6. Twist 3 sheets of foil to make separate spoons. Place a pinch of each powder in each spoon.
7. Ask an adult to light the candle. Hold each spoon over the flame using the clothespin as a handle. Record your observations on the chart.

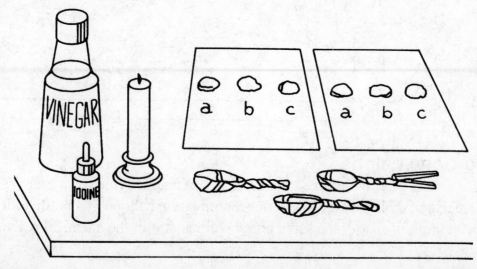

How Can You Identify a Chemical Reaction?, page 2

Chemical Reactions

Application of	Changes in powders		
	A	B	C
Vinegar			
Iodine			
Heat			

Drawing Conclusions

1. What changes did you observe when you put vinegar on each of the powders?
2. What changes did you observe when you put iodine on each of the powders?
3. What happened when the powders were heated?
4. In which test did a chemical reaction take place? How did you know?

MORE IDEAS

1. Include your setup and chart in your display.
2. Do research on other kinds of chemical reactions. Include your findings in your report.

What Is Combustion?

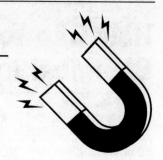

Combustion, or burning, is a chemical reaction that gives off heat and light. Oxygen (usually in the air), fuel, and heat are all needed for combustion to take place. If one of these is removed, combustion stops. In this project, you will investigate what happens to a fire when its available oxygen is used up.

MATERIALS

matches
1 candle (in a holder)
1 clear glass jar taller than the candle
    and wider than the base of the
    candle holder

CAUTION: Fire is dangerous. Do this project only in the presence of an adult.

Procedure

1. Light the candle, and allow it to burn for several seconds.
2. Turn the jar upside down, and carefully lower it over the candle.
3. Observe what happens.

Carefully lower the jar over the candle.

Drawing Conclusions

1. What happened to the candle flame?
2. Why do you think this occurred?
3. What happened to the oxygen in the jar?

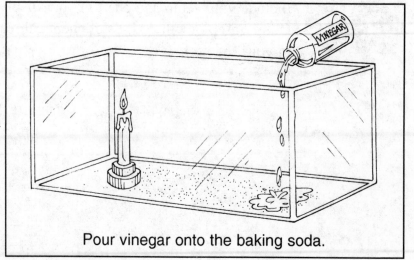

Pour vinegar onto the baking soda.

MORE IDEAS

1. Include your setup and findings with your display.
2. Investigate the property of combustion further by placing the candle in its holder at one end of an empty aquarium (see the illustration). Sprinkle baking soda (bicarbonate of soda) over the base of the aquarium, and light the candle. Pour half a cup of vinegar into one corner of the aquarium. Watch what happens to the candle as oxygen (air) is forced out of the aquarium by the carbon dioxide gas.

Name _____   Date _____

What Substance Is Needed for Burning?

Air is a mixture made of several gases. Oxygen is one of those gases. It takes fuel, oxygen, and heat to make a fire burn. The oxygen changes the fuel into a different kind of gas.

MATERIALS

clay	matches
water	short candle
goggles	clock with second hand
pie tin	quart jar
pint jar	gallon jar

CAUTION: This experiment must be done with an adult. Goggles must be worn.

Candle Burning Time

Jar	Time
Pint	
Quart	
Gallon	

Procedure

1. Put the clay in the pie tin. Stand the candle in the clay. Fill the pie tin with water. Then, ask an adult to light the candle.
2. Turn the pint jar upside down and set it over the candle. Watch the second hand on the clock to see how long it takes the flame to go out. Record the time in the chart.
3. Repeat Step 2 using the quart jar.
4. Repeat Step 2 using the gallon jar.

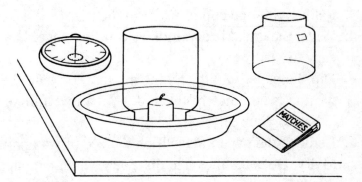

Drawing Conclusions

1. What substance was used up first, the candle wax or the oxygen in the jar?
2. Which substance controlled the reaction?
3. Based on your chart, predict the burning time of a candle in a half-pint volume of air.
4. Based on your chart, predict the burning time of a candle in a 10-gallon volume of air.
5. If your classroom holds about 50,000 gallons of air, how long would the candle burn?

Name _____   Date _____

How Can You Do Secret Writing?

Iodine combines with starch to form new compounds. Iodine is reddish-orange. Cornstarch is white. The new compound will be dark blue. You can use this information about iodine and cornstarch to send a secret message.

MATERIALS

iodine	measuring spoons
water	measuring cup
spoon	white paper
bowl	wax paper
cornstarch	toothpick
shallow pan	

CAUTION: This experiment must be done with an adult. Iodine is poisonous.

Procedure

1. In the bowl, mix together a tablespoon of cornstarch and a tablespoon of water. Stir until the mixture is smooth.
2. Use the toothpick as a pen. Use the cornstarch mixture as ink. Write a secret message on a piece of paper. Let the message dry.
3. While your message is drying, mix a tablespoon of iodine with one cup of water in the pan.
4. When the "ink" is dry, look at your message. Is it easy to read?
5. Dip the paper into the iodine mixture. Be sure the writing is completely covered. Wait a few minutes. What do you see?
6. Remove the paper. Place it on a piece of wax paper to dry. Does the message disappear when the paper dries? Explain.

The iodine combined with starches in both the paper and the cornstarch mixture. The paper and the cornstarch contain different kinds and amounts of starches. Therefore, they did not turn the same shade of blue when they reacted with the iodine.

Name _____ Date _____

What Are Acids and Bases?

Compounds can be divided into two groups: acids and bases. Lemon juice is an example of an acid. Baking soda is an example of a base. Some substances are neither acids nor bases. They are neutral.

Litmus paper can be used to discover whether a compound is an acid or a base. Litmus paper comes in colors of blue and pink. A substance that is a base will change pink litmus blue. A substance that is an acid will change blue litmus pink. If both strips stay the same color, the substance is neutral. It is neither a base nor an acid.

MATERIALS

lemon juice	pink and blue litmus paper
sugar water	carbonated drink
dish soap	5 small paper cups
milk	permanent marker

Procedure

1. Label each cup with the name of the substance. Pour a small amount of each substance into its cup.
2. Dip a strip of blue litmus into the first substance. Did it change color? Record your findings in the chart.
3. Dip a strip of pink litmus into the same cup. Did it change color? Record your findings in the chart.
4. Repeat steps 2 and 3 with each substance.

Testing Household Substances

Material	Reaction to blue litmus paper	Reaction to pink litmus paper
Lemon juice		
Milk		
Dish soap		
Sugar water		
Carbonated drink		

Drawing Conclusions

Which substances are acids? Which are neutral? Which is a base? Explain.

What Is a Solution?

A solution is formed when one substance (a solid, liquid, or gas) dissolves in another substance (a solid, liquid, or gas). The substance that dissolves is called the solute. The substance it dissolves in is called the solvent.

Water is the most common solvent, but it will not dissolve all substances. Several factors influence whether or not a solute dissolves. One is the temperature of the solvent. In this project, you will investigate the dissolving rates of sugar at different temperatures.

MATERIALS

ice	1 glass, size 10 oz. or larger
water	1 cup of sugar
1 teaspoon	thermometer
record sheet	

Procedure

1. Put 8 oz. of ice water into the glass.
2. Place 1 teaspoon of sugar into the glass and stir. If all the sugar dissolves, add another teaspoon and stir.
3. Continue to add sugar, 1 teaspoon at a time, until no more sugar will dissolve. Record how many teaspoons of sugar the ice water dissolved.
4. Empty the glass and wash it.
5. Repeat the experiment several times, using different temperatures of water. Record the temperatures.

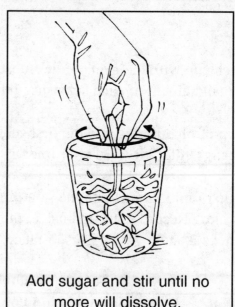

Add sugar and stir until no more will dissolve.

Drawing Conclusions

1. What did you discover about the amount of sugar that would dissolve at different temperatures? What happened as the water temperatures rose?
2. What do you think would happen if you used very hot water?

MORE IDEAS

1. Include your setup and findings in your display.
2. Try using other solids, such as mints, chocolate drops, or salt, as your solute. Try other liquids, such as vinegar or a carbonated drink, as your solvent. Remember to change only one variable at a time.

What Is Chromatography?

Chromatography is a way of separating various dissolved substances in a mixture. Paper chromatography is based on the fact that porous paper absorbs various dissolved substances at different speeds and therefore, in a given time, to different extents. In this project, you will investigate paper chromatography as you separate substances from various mixtures.

MATERIALS

several pencils or sticks   masking tape
several coffee filters or paper towels   scissors
several clear plastic cups   water
several colored markers

Procedure

1. Cut a coffee filter or paper towel into strips approximately 1.5 in. (35 mm) wide—one strip for each cup. Cut each strip about 1.5 in. (35 mm) shorter than the height of the cups. CAUTION: Be careful when handling the scissors.

2. Using the markers, make a large dot near one end of the strips (a different color on each strip), and allow the ink to dry.

3. Tape the other end of each strip to a pencil or stick.

4. Place about 2 in. (5 cm) of water in the bottom of each cup, and lower the colored ends of the strips into the water. (The paper should barely touch the water. Adjust the water level if necessary.) The colored dots must not be allowed to touch the water.

5. Set the pencils or sticks across the rims of the cups to hold up the strips of paper.

6. Allow the strips to remain in place for about an hour. Observe the movement of the colors up the strips.

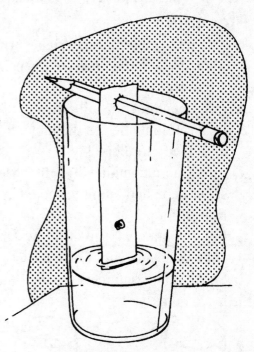

Leave the strips for about an hour.

Drawing Conclusions

1. Where did the bands of color come from?
2. Why do you think the colors rose to different levels on the paper strips?

MORE IDEAS

1. Try using other liquids (such as nail polish remover or rubbing alcohol) and compare the results. CAUTION: The fumes from nail polish remover are dangerous.
2. Try using different types of pens to make the colored dots.

How Can the Rate at Which a Substance Dissolves Be Changed?

A solution is a mixture of two or more substances. A solution is made of two parts. The solute is the substance being dissolved in a solution. The solvent is the substance that dissolves the solute. Do this experiment to learn more about solutions.

MATERIALS

6 plastic containers of the
    same size, with lids
hot water
tap water
6 sugar cubes

Procedure

1. You will perform three trials during this experiment. Read the experiment directions. Then, look at the chart on the next page. Fill in your predictions for each trial before you start Step 2.
2. Fill 2 containers $\frac{2}{3}$ full of water. Drop 1 sugar cube into each cup. Cap each container.
3. Leave 1 container on the table. Shake the other container. Record which sugar cube dissolved more quickly.
4. Fill 2 more containers $\frac{2}{3}$ full of water. Drop a whole cube into 1 container. Crush a second sugar cube and add it to the other container. Cap each container.
5. Repeat Step 3.
6. Fill 1 container $\frac{2}{3}$ full of hot water and another container $\frac{2}{3}$ full of tap water. Drop a sugar cube into each cup. Cap each container.
7. Shake both containers for the same length of time. Record which sugar cube dissolved more quickly.

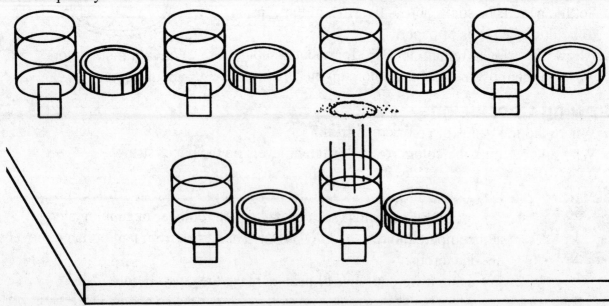

Name _____   Date _____

How Can the Rate at Which a Substance Dissolves Be Changed?, page 2

Dissolving Sugar

Trial	Sugar cubes	Predicted outcome	Outcome
1	Unshaken or shaken		
2	Whole or crushed		
3	Warm or cold water		

Drawing Conclusions

1. Were your predictions correct?
2. Which factors made the sugar cubes dissolve faster?
3. How does changing the solvent in Trial 3 make a solute dissolve more quickly?
4. How can you change a solute so it dissolves more quickly?

MORE IDEAS

1. Include your setup and findings with your display.
2. Try using other solutes and solvents. What do you find? Include your findings in your report.

What Is Distillation?

Distillation is a process that separates a mixture into the liquids or solids of which it is made. Distillation usually involves the change of a substance into a vapor that is then condensed to its liquid form. In this project, you will investigate ways to extract (distill) water from a mixture.

MATERIALS

1 glass or cup,
   shorter than the pan
2 small, clean rocks
   (scrub them if necessary)
1 large piece of clear plastic, large
   enough to cover the top of the pan or tub

water
sand
salt
masking tape
1 large pan or tub

Procedure

1. Set the pan in a sunny spot outdoors.
2. Mix $\frac{1}{2}$ cup of salt and $\frac{1}{2}$ cup of sand with enough water to fill the pan about 2 in. (5 cm) deep.
3. Place the glass in the center of the pan, and place a rock in the glass to weigh it down enough to stand in the water.
4. Cover the pan with the plastic. Pull the plastic tightly and tape it to the pan.
5. Place the other rock in the center of the plastic, directly over the glass. This will make an indentation in the plastic over the glass. Do not allow the plastic to touch the glass.
6. Wait several hours and check the glass. If no water has collected in the glass, allow more time or add another rock to the center of the plastic to increase the indentation.
7. Once water has collected in the glass, remove it from the pan, hold it up, and look at it.

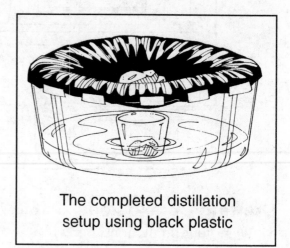

The completed distillation setup using black plastic

Drawing Conclusions

1. Does the water in the glass appear clear?
2. Taste just a drop. Is it salty? Why or why not?

MORE IDEAS

1. Include your setup and results in your display.
2. Try using black plastic instead of clear plastic to cover the pan. With black plastic, does water collect in the glass faster or slower than with clear plastic? Why do you think this is so?

Name _____ Date _____

What Is Archimedes' Principle?

Archimedes was an ancient Greek physicist, mathematician, and inventor. He discovered that when a solid object is immersed in a liquid, it is pushed up in the liquid by a force equal to the weight of the liquid it displaced. The weight of the liquid displaced is the same as the weight of the object. If the displaced water weighs more than the object, the object floats. If the displaced water weighs less than the object, the object sinks. When the object is immersed in the liquid, it weighs less than it does in air. In this project, you will investigate the displacement of water.

MATERIALS

1 pencil (The six-sided type with flat edges works best.)
2 identical plastic cups containing equal amounts of water
12-in. (30-cm) ruler
masking tape

Procedure

1. Tape the pencil to the table to hold it steady.
2. Balance the ruler across the pencil.
3. Place a cup of water on each end of the ruler until it is again balanced.
4. Dip one finger into one of the cups. Be sure you do not touch the cup. Observe what happens to the water level in that cup.
5. Observe the balance of the ruler.
6. Balance the two cups again. This time dip two fingers deeper into the water. Observe the water level and the balance of the ruler.

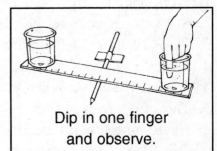

Dip in one finger and observe.

Drawing Conclusions

1. Why did the water level rise when you dipped your finger in?
2. What happened to the balance and the water level as you dipped your fingers deeper into the water?
3. Why do you think this happened?

Fill the glass with different liquids.

MORE IDEAS

1. Include your setup and observations with your display.
2. Observe what happens when you place objects made of different materials in different liquids. Into a tall glass, carefully pour, one after the other, corn syrup, mineral oil, cooking oil, salt water (containing a little food coloring), and rubbing alcohol. Notice how the liquids settle in the glass. Carefully drop in small objects, such as an eraser, a piece of wood, and a small plastic toy. Note where each object floats.

Name _____   Date _____

How Can You Compare the Inertia of Two Objects?

Inertia is a property of matter by which it remains in motion or at rest until acted upon by another force. The amount of matter in an object is its mass. More mass in an object also means that it has more inertia. More force will be needed to move it because it has a greater tendency to remain at rest. Try this experiment to learn more.

MATERIALS

rubber band   steel washer, 4–5 cm in diameter
30-cm metal strip   rock, 2–4 cm in diameter
3 books   clock with second hand

Procedure

1. Work with a partner. Use the rubber band to attach the washer to the metal strip.
2. Stack the 3 books on the edge of a table.
3. Place 10 cm of the strip underneath the books.
4. Push the washer end of the strip down about 5 cm. Have your partner look at the second hand of the clock. When your partner says "Go," let the strip go.
5. The strip moves quickly up and down. Each time it moves down, it makes one vibration. Have your partner time 10 seconds. Count the number of vibrations. When your partner says "Stop," record the number of vibrations in the chart.
6. Repeat Steps 4 and 5 two more times.
7. Find the average number of vibrations of the three trials.
8. Now, attach the small rock to the end of the strip. Repeat Steps 3 through 7.

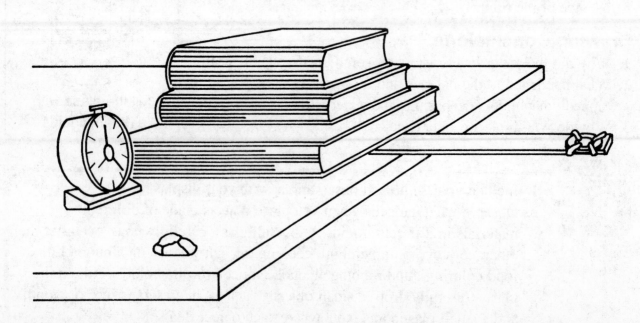

How Can You Compare the Inertia of Two Objects?, page 2

Inertia Comparison

Metal strip with washer	Vibrations per 10 seconds	Metal strip with rock	Vibrations per 10 seconds
Trial 1		Trial 1	
Trial 2		Trial 2	
Trial 3		Trial 3	
Total		Total	
Average		Average	

Drawing Conclusions

1. What was the average number of vibrations for the strip with the washer?
2. What was the average number of vibrations for the strip with the rock?
3. Was it easier for the strip to move the washer or the rock? Why?
4. Which object had greater inertia? Why?
5. Which object had greater mass? Why?

MORE IDEAS

1. Include your setup and chart in your display.
2. Do research to find different kinds of forces that can affect inertia.
3. Do research on space travel. Is inertia the same in space? Would you need more or less force to affect inertia in space?

Name _____ Date _____

What Are Balanced and Unbalanced Forces?

Some forces result in movement, and some do not. Two forces that are equal in size but opposite in direction are balanced forces. Balanced forces do not change the position of an object. To cause a change in motion, forces must be unbalanced. Unbalanced forces are opposite and unequal. Do this experiment to learn more about these forces.

MATERIALS

tissue paper
empty squeezable detergent bottle
small paper cup
water

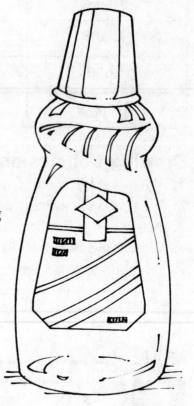

Procedure

1. Moisten a small piece of tissue paper, and shape it into a plug for the hole in the top of the bottle. Place it in the hole to plug the bottle.
2. Place the cup upside down over the bottle.
3. Squeeze the bottle as hard as you can. Observe what happens.

Drawing Conclusions

1. What two forces were acting to cause what you observed?
2. How did the two forces compare in their direction and size?
3. Could balanced forces have caused what you observed? Explain.

MORE ✓ **IDEAS**

1. Include your setup in your display. Demonstrate the experiment for the judges.
2. Do more research on balanced and unbalanced forces. Include your findings in your report.

What Do Newton's Laws Have to Do with Seatbelt Laws?

No one goes to court to argue about Newton's First Law of Motion. It's not that kind of law. When you are riding in a car and someone brakes hard, your body continues to move forward. Young children can be thrown much farther than adults because they are so light. This is the reason that laws require children to ride buckled in car seats. This activity demonstrates Newton's First Law and the need for seatbelts.

MATERIALS

books	a board at least 1 meter long
a toy car	1 small stone
ruler	1 heavy stone

Procedure

1. Make a ramp by putting one end of the board on a pile of books. Put another book at the bottom of the ramp to act as a barrier.
2. Balance the small stone on top of the toy car. Let the car roll down the ramp.
3. Balance the large stone on top of the car, and let the car roll down the ramp again.

Drawing Conclusions

1. How far was the small stone thrown when the car hit the barrier?
2. How far was the large stone thrown?
3. Do you better understand the need for safety seats for children? Do you think seat belts are also important for adults? How would you explain this activity to someone else?

MORE IDEAS

1. Include your setup in your display. Do the activity for the judges.
2. Do research on traffic accidents. Do seatbelts really help to save lives?

How Does Mass Affect Acceleration?

Newton's Second Law of Motion states that an object accelerates faster as the force gets larger or as the mass of the object gets smaller. You can do this experiment to demonstrate Newton's law.

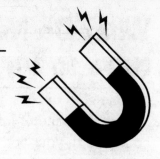

MATERIALS

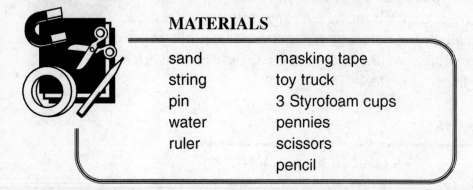

sand	masking tape
string	toy truck
pin	3 Styrofoam cups
water	pennies
ruler	scissors
	pencil

Procedure

1. Label the cups **A**, **B**, and **C**.
2. Punch a hole in the bottom of cup C using the pin. Make a pencil mark 1.5 cm up from the bottom of the cup on the inside. Tape the cup to the back of the toy truck.
3. Fill cup B with sand. Put the cup in the back of the truck.
4. Place the truck at one end of a table. Tie one end of the string to the front of the truck. Tie the other end through cup A.
5. Extend the string the length of the table. Let the string and cup drop 30 cm over the edge of the table.
6. Drop some pennies into cup A until the truck moves.

7. Move the truck back to the starting point. Fill cup C with water up to the pencil mark. Let the truck go. Measure the distance between the drops of water that fall to the table from the hole in the bottom of the cup. Record it on the chart.

8. Return the truck to the starting point. Untape cup C from the truck, empty the cup, and retape it to the back of the truck. Dry the top of the table.

9. Remove the pennies from cup A. Be sure the empty cup still hangs over the edge of the table.

10. Remove the sand-filled cup B from the truck. Repeat Steps 6 and 7.

Measuring Acceleration

Truck	Distance between drops
With sand	
Without sand	

Drawing Conclusions

1. What part of the experiment is the force?
2. What was the distance between the drops of water that fell from the truck carrying sand?
3. What was the distance between the drops of water that fell from the truck without sand?
4. Did the truck accelerate faster with the sand or without the sand? How do you know?
5. What caused the difference in acceleration?

MORE IDEAS

1. Include your setup and chart in your display. Demonstrate the experiment for the judges.
2. Do research on the launching of the space shuttle. How much acceleration is needed to break free from the Earth's gravitational pull?

Can You Observe the Direction of Opposite Forces?

Forces always occur together. When there is one force, whether an object is still or moving, there is another force working in the opposite direction—a reaction. Newton's Third Law of Motion states that for every action, there is an equal and opposite reaction. Do this experiment to see Newton's law in action.

MATERIALS

scissors   an empty 1-quart milk carton
tape   sink or tub filled with water 5 cm deep
balloon

Procedure

1. Cut the milk carton in half lengthwise. Cut a small notch in the bottom of the milk carton.
2. Blow up the balloon. Pinch it closed with your fingers, but do not tie it.
3. Put the balloon in the milk carton, placing the end you are holding into the notch.
4. Tape the balloon securely into the milk carton as shown below.
5. Put the carton in a tub of water.
6. Release the balloon so the air flows out of the balloon.

Drawing Conclusions

1. Which way did the air coming out of the balloon move? Which way did the carton move?
2. Which force was the action force?
3. Which force was the reaction force?
4. What scientific law did you observe in this activity?
5. How is the force of the air in the balloon like a propeller in a boat?

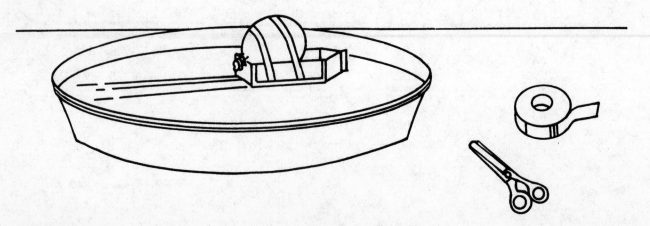

Name _____   Date _____

Do Pulleys Make Work Easier?

A pulley is made by wrapping a rope around a wheel. The wheel has a track around it to hold the rope in place. A pulley that does not move is called a fixed pulley. It makes work easier because it changes the direction of the force. A moveable pulley is fastened to the load. As the rope moves, the pulley and the load both move. Movable pulleys make work easier by reducing the force. Do this experiment to see how pulleys help.

MATERIALS

pail	sand	spring scale
meter stick	string	small pulley

Procedure

1. Fill the pail $\frac{1}{4}$ full with sand.
2. Lift the pail with the spring scale. Record the force needed to lift the pail.
3. Place the meter stick across two desks. Then, tie one end of the string to the meter stick. Run the string through the pulley. Tie the free end of the string to the scale.
4. Hook the pail onto the pulley. Pull on the scale to lift the pail. Record the force in the chart.

Force for Lifting Pail

Step	Force
2	
4	

Drawing Conclusions

1. What kind of pulley system did you use?
2. What force was needed to lift the pail in Step 2?
3. What force was needed in Step 4?
4. How does using a pulley help make lifting an object easier?

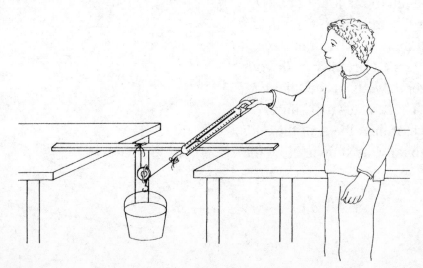

Name _____   Date _____

How Can You Compare Forces?

It takes force to lift something. The force needed to lift an object is equal to the weight of the object. You can compare the amount of force needed to lift various objects. To do this, you can make a special kind of lever.

MATERIALS

knitting needle
long cardboard tube (from paper towel or plastic wrap)
small objects such as marbles, paper clips, and keys
shoe box   ruler
pencil   quarter
penny   scissors

Procedure

1. Measure the length of the shoe box and divide by 2 to find the middle of the box. On the side of the box, mark the midpoint with your pencil. Then measure down 3 cm from the top of the box. Make a mark, as shown.

2. Do the same thing to the opposite side of the shoe box. The marks should be exactly opposite each other.

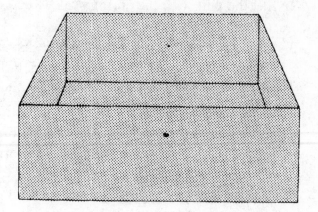

3. Carefully push the knitting needle all the way through the box at both of these marks. Then take the needle out and set it aside. Now you have a stand for your lever.

4. Check that the cardboard tube fits lengthwise in the shoe box. If the tube is too long, cut off enough to make it fit easily.

5. Measure the cardboard tube to find the center point and mark it. Mark the opposite side of the tube, also. Carefully push your needle through both walls of the tube and then remove it. This creates a channel through the sides of the tube. Cut the ends of the tube diagonally, as shown. Now the lever has pans.

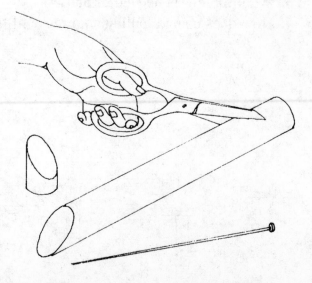

How Can You Compare Forces?, page 2

6. Hold the tube inside the box with the short ends up as shown. Push the needle through the hole on one side of the shoe box, through the cardboard tube, and through the opposite side of the shoe box. Now you have a lever balance.

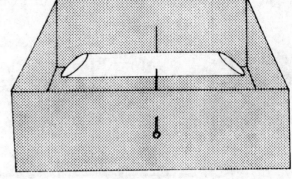

7. Place the quarter in the right-hand pan. What happens to the tube? What force is pushing the right-hand pan down?

8. Place a penny in the left-hand pan. What happens to the levels of the two pans? What causes the change?

9. Compare the amount of force applied by the different small objects you collected. Then, make a list of the objects. At the top of the list, write the object that exerts the most force. At the bottom, write the object that exerts the least force. Write the rest of the objects in order between these two.

Drawing Conclusions

1. What is the fulcrum? What is the lever?
2. Which exerts more force: the penny or quarter? How can you tell?
3. What would happen if you changed the location of the fulcrum? What would happen if you made the lever longer or shorter?

Can You Make a Magnet?

Magnets attract objects made of iron, nickel, and cobalt. The forces are strongest at their poles, or ends. Some metals can become like a magnet. You can make your own magnet. Here's how.

MATERIALS

candle with holder	3 iron nails
matches	paper clips
bar magnet	pliers
hammer	

CAUTION: This activity must be supervised by an adult.

Procedure

1. Stroke one of the iron nails with the pole of the magnet in one direction only.
2. Try to pick up the paper clips with the nail.
3. Remove the clips. Then, hammer along the length of the nail several times. Try to pick up the clips again.
4. Repeat Steps 1 and 2 with another nail. Remove the clips.
5. Stroke the nail with the pole of the magnet in both directions. Try to pick up the clips again.
6. Repeat Steps 1 and 2 with another nail. Then, remove the clips.
7. Hold the nail with the pliers, and place the nail in the flame of a candle for about 3 minutes. Try to pick up the clips again.

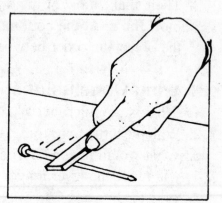

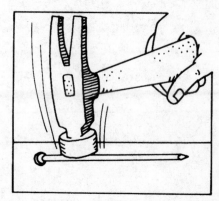

Drawing Conclusions

1. How did you make the nails act like magnets?
2. What happened to the nails after you hammered or heated them?
3. What happened to the nail after rubbing it with the magnet in both directions?
4. What are three ways in which magnetism can be destroyed?

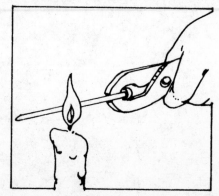

Name _____ Date _____

How Do Nonmagnetic Materials Affect a Magnet?

Materials made of metal, such as iron, nickel, and cobalt, are attracted by a magnet. In this activity, you will find out if nonmagnetic materials affect a magnetic field.

MATERIALS

a paper clip	string 37 cm (15 in.) long
waxed paper	block of wood
alnico magnet	ring stand with test-tube holder
cloth	squares of paper
iron nail	aluminum foil

Procedure

1. Set up the materials as shown in the drawing.
2. Pass the squares of paper through the space between the clip and the pole of the magnet. Record your results in the chart.
3. Pass the foil, cloth, waxed paper, and nail through the space.
4. Repeat the experiment with the poles reversed.

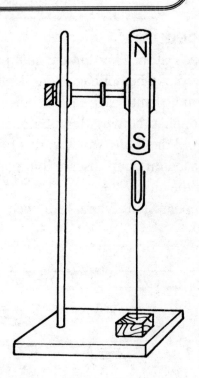

Drawing Conclusions

1. Why is the paper clip held in place?
2. What happened in Step 2? Explain.
3. Did any of the materials affect the magnetic field? Why?
4. What happened when you reversed the bar magnet so the N pole pointed down? Explain.

Magnetic Attraction

Material	Effect
paper	
foil	
cloth	
waxed paper	
nail	

Is It a Conductor or an Insulator?

A conductor is a material that allows a current to flow through it easily. An insulator is a material that keeps a current from moving through it. Do this experiment to find conductors and insulators.

MATERIALS

3 pieces of insulated copper wire,
    each 30 cm long and stripped back
      about 2.5 cm on each end
pencil, sharpened on each end
light bulb in socket
sheet of aluminum foil

D-size battery
screwdriver
door key
sheet of paper
penny
rubber band

Procedure

1. Look at the chart on the next page. Read the list of objects in the "Item Tested" column. Predict whether each item is an insulator or a conductor. Record your predictions before you go on to Step 2.
2. Connect the wire, light bulb, and battery as shown in the picture.
3. Hold the 2 uncovered ends of the wires to the foil. Observe the result.
4. Based on your observation, place a check in either the "conductor" or "insulator" column in the chart.
5. Repeat Steps 3 and 4 for each item listed in the chart.

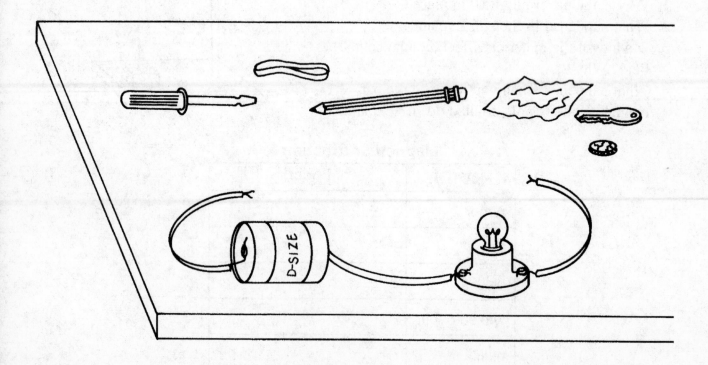

Is It a Conductor or an Insulator?, page 2

Conductors and Insulators

Item Tested	Prediction	Conductor	Insulator
Aluminum foil			
Door key			
Paper			
Penny			
Rubber band			
Pencil			

Drawing Conclusions

1. Which items were conductors?
2. Which items were insulators?
3. Which of your predictions were correct? Which were not correct?
4. What kinds of materials make good conductors?

MORE IDEAS

1. Include your setup and chart with your display.
2. Choose more items to test. Make your prediction, then test the item.
3. Do research to find what kind of conductors and insulators are used most in electrical work. Include your findings in your report.

What Is a Fuse?

As electric current flows, wires and other objects in the circuit may get too hot. They can cause the circuit to short and change the flow of electricity. A fuse is made with a wire that melts if the current gets too hot. Here's how to make a fuse.

MATERIALS

2 dry cells	scissors	aluminum foil
2 paper clips	ruler	screwdriver with insulated handle
wooden block	wire	2 thumbtacks
light bulb in socket		

CAUTION: This activity must be supervised by an adult.

Procedure

1. Place each paper clip against the underside of a thumbtack. Press the thumbtacks into the wooden block as shown. The tacks should be about 3 cm apart and upright against the wood.
2. Place a strip of aluminum foil about 5 cm long by 1 cm wide between the clips.
3. Remove some insulation from two of the wires so that the circuit can be set up as shown in Figure B.
4. Set up the dry cells, wire, and bulb as shown.
5. While holding the insulated handle of the screwdriver, carefully touch the metal to the two stripped wires. Observe what happens to the aluminum.

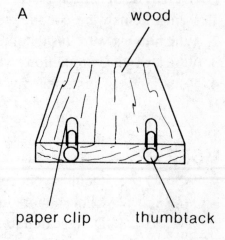

A

wood

paper clip   thumbtack

B

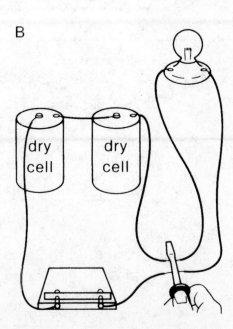

dry cell   dry cell

Drawing Conclusions

1. How did you short the circuit?
2. Did the current travel back to the source through the bulb or the screwdriver?
3. What happened to the foil? Why?
4. Why is a fuse helpful in a circuit?

What Is a Series Circuit?

A resistor is a device that uses electrical energy because it resists the flow of energy. A light bulb is an example of a resistor. When a circuit has two or more resistors and the electrical current flows in one direction, it is called a series circuit. In this kind of circuit, the flow of electricity stays the same. The resistors must share the flow, so they may not be able to work to full capacity.

MATERIALS

2 light bulbs in sockets
4 pieces of insulated copper wire,
    each 30 cm long and stripped back
    about 2.5 cm on each end

1.5 volt dry cell
screwdriver
switch

Procedure

1. Create a series circuit by connecting the wires as follows:
   - join one terminal of the dry cell to a light bulb
   - join the first light bulb to the second one
   - join the second light bulb to the switch
   - join the switch to the remaining dry cell terminal.
2. Close the switch, then open it. Observe the results.
3. Unscrew one light bulb. Observe the results.
4. Close the switch, then open it. Observe the results.

Drawing Conclusions

1. What happened when you closed the switch the first time?
2. What happened when you closed the switch after you unscrewed one light bulb?
3. Through how many paths can an electric current flow in a series circuit? How do you know?

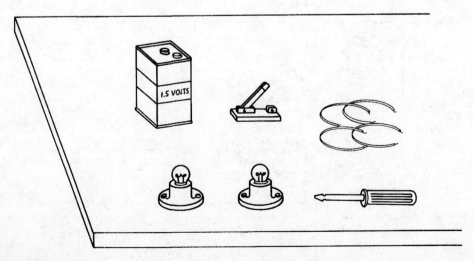

What Is a Parallel Circuit?

A parallel circuit has more than one path that an electric current can travel through. These circuits usually have a fuse or circuit breaker joined to them to keep the wires from getting too hot.

MATERIALS

3 light bulbs in sockets
7 pieces of insulated copper wire,
    each 30 cm long and stripped back
    about 2.5 cm on each end

screwdriver
1.5 volt dry cell
switch

Procedure

1. Create a parallel circuit by connecting the wires as follows:
   • join one terminal of the dry cell to a light bulb
   • join the first light bulb to the second bulb
   • join the second light bulb to the third bulb
   • join the bulbs in the reverse order to the switch
   • join the switch to the remaining dry cell terminal.
2. Close the switch, then open it. Observe the results.
3. Unscrew one light bulb.
4. Close the switch, then open it. Observe the results.

Drawing Conclusions

1. What happened when you closed the switch the first time?
2. What happened when you closed the switch the second time?
3. Through how many paths can an electric current flow in a parallel circuit? How do you know?
4. What is the difference between a series circuit and a parallel circuit? What kind is used in home electrical wiring?